A7M
REl

REFUGEE
RADIO
TIMES

REFUGEE RADIO TIMES

Voices of Asylum, Identity and Resistance

Edited by
Lorna Stephenson &
Stephen Silverwood

Refugee Radio Times
Published by **Refugee Radio**
Registered charity: 1133554
www.refugeeradio.org.uk

This edition 2014
Copyright © Refugee Radio 2014
First printed June 2014

ISBN-13: 978-0-9929374-0-9

Text edited by Lorna Stephenson
Book design and project management by Stephen Silverwood

CONTENTS

ACKNOWLEDGEMENTS

This book was produced as a collaborative process between two groups of people. The first was made up of refugees, asylum seekers and other migrants who had stories that they wanted to tell. The second group consisted of journalists and writers who wanted to help them tell those stories. Our book would not have been possible without both sides teaming up to work together.

If integration is a two-way process then it is incumbent on the host population to communicate with their new neighbours and to build a new community together. Rather than a debate about refugees and migrants, we wanted to create a debate *by* refugees and migrants. So we are grateful to those who enabled the mentoring project that led to the creation of this book.

We would like to thank all of the contributors and we would especially like to thank the volunteers who gave their time to make this project happen: in particular Meriel Beattie and Derek Parkinson who worked so diligently to support their mentees.

Special thanks must also go to our families and loved ones who supported us and put up with us during the production of this book.

Refugee Radio is an independent charity with no government funding and we would like to thank all of our supporters, funders and donors over the years. We would also like to thank the Big Lottery Fund: Awards for All England for agreeing to fund this project and for supporting our vision for the Refugee Radio Times.

INTRODUCTION

In this chapter, **Stephen Silverwood** *reveals the hidden history behind the creation of the Refugee Radio charity and uncovers some of the truths behind popular asylum myths.*

I was a pirate radio DJ...

If this evokes images of late-night excitement and urban danger then the marketing has paid off. The reality, however, was quite different. It involved a lot more tatty squats and stolen equipment, for a start.

I started out in radio with my mates, Andy and Matty, with the intention of doing a weekly show to promote gigs for our band. We were an unsigned electro-punk trio, playing shows at every dingy bar and venue from Brighton to London. If it had a Hell's Angel for a doorman and a sticky carpet, then we'd played it. If it had a broken PA controlled by a deaf soundman, we'd played it. If it had a urinal you could see from the bar, we'd played it. You get the picture...

We were hoping to take our act to new audiences and a pirate radio show seemed like a great opportunity. It was on FM as well as the internet so, in theory, anyone could be listening.

In reality, though, it was usually just our mates tuning in to listen to us playing Spacemen 3 records and bickering with each other.

There was a fair amount of clandestine subterfuge, though. The radio studio was permanently on the move to avoid detection by the authorities. We would get a text message telling us this week's new location and would have just an hour to dash across town in search of whatever random dive it had relocated to this time.

But all good things come to an end. Eventually someone stole our transmitter. We like to think it was the police busting the station but, in reality, it was probably just stolen for scrap. This forced us to move to a new system where each DJ would broadcast from the safety of their own home, using their computers to stream the music. The band broke up too, so we each started doing a show by ourselves. I would spend most of my show blasting punk and reggae numbers, "humorously" teasing my former bandmates with impromptu theme-nights.

One evening soon after, I had a friend round to visit. It happened to be the night of my show and so I invited him to join me on air and play some tunes. His name was Heval and he was a Kurdish refugee from Syria. I knew him as an interpreter and musician, having met him through the course of my day job for the Money Advice & Community Support Service.

That night we were just drinking beer and playing Eminem. I didn't think anything of it at first. And then we started talking about all of the negative stereotyping and discrimination in the media against refugees and asylum seekers. Tabloids such as the Daily Mail and The Sun were routinely publishing headlines like "Asylum Seekers Attack Britain" and "Swan Bake", accusing asylum seekers of scrounging benefits and eating swans. These stories were often untrue, but the papers published them day after day in a relentless campaign that reminded me of the persecution of Jews and Gypsies in Nazi Germany, or Tutsis in Rwanda. I had known a Kosovan refugee in London who had his flat fire-bombed by neighbours and an Afghan child who had been run over by racist thugs. It felt like there was no way for them to resist this propaganda about them, no way for the scapegoats to respond to the media misinformation... And then I realised: we were the media too. We had the airwaves. We could give them a voice. I left my job at Money Advice and formed Refugee Radio the day after I left.

It was a deliberate choice to call it "Refugee" Radio, as I wanted to reclaim the word as a positive thing and to resist the new-speak of "asylum seeker", which had emerged laden with negative connotations. I wanted to support people not to feel ashamed of being a refugee and to feel comfortable to identify as a refugee even if they had not been given formal refugee status in the law. It was to become something of a barrier for some people, though, and keeping it was an example of my personal belligerence.

The original Board of Trustees consisted of myself and Heval, plus three professionals who were working with the refugee community: the human rights solicitor Christianne Silverwood; the social worker Zoe Rosenfield; and the founder of the Migrant English Project, Gianpaolo Boldrini. Over time the board has expanded to also include more

people who have been through the immigration
system themselves and can represent the
communities we work with.

My first programmes were recorded using a
microphone I bought at the Pound Shop and were
broadcast on our local community radio station,
RadioReverb. The quality of the audio was never
great but I was more interested in helping people to
tell their stories than in making a slick radio show.
Some people will say the sound quality has not
improved much over the last six years, either, but
over that time there have been hundreds of people on
the show and all of them have experienced the power
of being able to speak directly to their new
community. I have also managed to get the show onto
other stations, including the likes of Resonance FM,
Refugee Week Radio, Radio 1812, Radio Free
Brighton, Afghan Voice Radio and Homely Planet
Radio. They may not sound as cool as pirate radio,
but they do have the added bonus of not having their
transmitters stolen for scrap metal.

Many of those programmes are still available to
download as podcasts or to stream from our website,
including one very early interview with Heval, where
he played traditional Kurdish music on the tamboura
live in the studio. That got me thinking again... I
realised that music has always been part of the
process of cultural integration and negotiation for
new migrant communities. When I was a child it was
the record label, Two Tone, and the sound of second-
wave ska forging an unlikely new hybrid out of
rudeboy and skinhead subcultures in bands like The
Specials. Then, when I was a bit older, it was the
Asian Underground fusion of reggae and hiphop

bringing Indian and West Indian kids together in bands like Asian Dub Foundation. I started to wonder: would it be possible to do something similar with refugee and asylum seeker musicians?

I then formed the Refugee Radio Orchestra as another project, bringing together a group of disparate artists including a reggae guitarist from Burundi, a crooner from Iran, a rapper from Nigeria and a dancer from the Congo. It was a great success and produced some fantastic music, culminating in a performance at the Glastonbury Festival. Unfortunately, this triumph coincided with the economic downturn and the unprecedented slashing of the national Arts Council budget. The Refugee Radio Orchestra was not able to continue but it had given me the taste for new projects within the Refugee Radio umbrella.

Now I continue to make the weekly radio programme as always, but alongside that I also run a number of separate community projects including the Community Resilience Project, which supports refugees with mental health issues. I also started a mentoring project where refugees and asylum seekers who were interested in writing would be matched with experienced journalists and writers to help them develop chapters for the very book you are now holding in your hands. This has been a very worthwhile project and I have met some brilliant new people along the way, including contributors like Eleanor, Farah, Robert, Ivo, Gharghasht and Husnu; volunteer mentors like Meriel and Derek; and our editor for this book, Lorna Stephenson.

Lorna was responsible for the task of editing the text in this book, which meant creating a thematic structure and then working closely with the contributors in their storytelling journey as well as copy-writing and proof-reading and editing the text of every chapter. It also meant writing her own chapters and conducting field research and interviews out on the streets in Calais. Lorna first came to Refugee Radio as a volunteer to produce the first issue of our magazine and this entire project would not have been thinkable if we were not fortunate enough to have her on the team.

This book includes a range of perspectives on the issues of asylum, refuge and migration. There are firsthand accounts of flight from conflict, such as Eleanor's childhood memories of Burma (page 1); flight from oppression in Iran and sanctuary for religious freedoms in the UK (page 57). There are two accounts of political persecution in Cameroon (page 87) that also cover arriving in the UK as an asylum seeker and the experience of being imprisoned in immigration detention. One of the firsthand accounts is by someone who is still trying to reach the UK from the makeshift camps of Calais (page 17). These balance the positive and negative aspects of the journeys involved.

The book also covers the inner journeys and struggles of migration. Gharghasht examines the identity crisis of Afghans living in the diaspora through his own experiences (page 123). Other chapters tackle the psychological effects of dislocation and trauma. Husnu writes about his own recovery from the Post-Traumatic Stress Disorder caused by torture in his home country and exacerbated by the asylum system (page 33) and elsewhere he interviews a leading trauma-expert for more answers (page 43). Nina looks in detail at the impact of refugee trauma initiatives through a series of personal case studies (page 101).

In my later chapter, I explore the absurdity of the asylum process through reflecting my own experiences as a refugee advice worker with the writings of the Czech novelist, Franz Kafka (page 71). In her conclusion, Lorna asks whether migrant voices can be heard in the asylum system and looks to the growing grassroots movements in support of migrant rights (page 139).

This has been a productive experience so far but the myths and misinformation are still out there, though, and no matter how many radio programmes we make, they still get perpetuated. There are so many myths in circulation but, after seven years of running Refugee Radio, these are my personal top seven:

Refugee Radio's Top Seven Asylum and Refugee Myths:

Myth: Asylum Seekers eat swans.
Busted: This never happened.

The Sun newspaper first splashed the story across its front page in July 2003 and then again in February 2008. The articles variously blame "callous asylum seekers" and then "Eastern European poachers" as if the two were the same thing (they are not). The paper claimed that police had issued a statement saying they had arrested two members of a gang. In fact, there were never any arrests and the police never issued any statement. The Swan Sanctuary quoted in the paper saying swans are a "delicacy" to Eastern Europeans also denied issuing such a statement.

So no arrests, no gang and no barbecued swan, then? What actually happened? Well, the truth was that a member of the public phoned the Swan Sanctuary to say they had seen someone pushing a swan in a shopping trolley. That's all. Other newspapers, including The Telegraph, have accused The Sun of making the rest of the story up themselves, including the part about asylum seekers being involved and the part about people eating the swans (i.e. the entire story).

The Press Complaints Commission eventually found that The Sun was "unable to provide any evidence for the story", and had presented it is a "factual account" when in fact it was mere fiction. In response The Sun printed a small "clarification" on page 41 of one edition admitting they couldn't be sure the people were asylum seekers. Considering the fact that the story had first appeared as a front page headline, this hardly counts as making amends, especially as the headline was subsequently picked up and repeated as fact by the Daily Mail and other publications around the world.

The myth: Asylum seekers come to the UK to scrounge welfare benefits.
Busted: Asylum seekers can't claim benefits.

Asylum seekers are not allowed to work or claim benefits. They can either live on any savings they have or apply to the Home Office for support. If they are approved for support they get a small amount of money every week. It is 70% of what you can get for Jobseeker's Allowance, so a third less than you need to live and well below the poverty line. They are not given mobile phones or free cars either.

Asylum seekers do not come to the UK to claim benefits. Most of them don't know anything about the welfare system when they leave their country.

The myth: Asylum seekers are illegal immigrants.
Busted: You can't be an illegal immigrant if you are an asylum seeker.

If you are an asylum seeker it means you have arrived in the UK and asked to claim asylum, either at the airport or port when you arrived or later at the Home Office. You have made yourself known to the authorities and you will have been fingerprinted, photographed and security-checked. You may be detained in an immigration removal centre or you may instead be asked to report to the Home Office every week or every month so they can keep track of you. You are here legally.

If the Home Office decide to refuse your claim, you will be a 'failed asylum seeker' and you will be asked to leave the UK. If they decide to accept your claim for asylum, you will become an officially recognised refugee and be allowed to stay in the UK permanently.

An 'illegal immigrant' is someone who has come to the UK and has never made themselves known to the authorities, or someone who has stayed in the UK longer than they were allowed to.

The myth: Most asylum seekers are bogus.
Busted: If you are refused asylum it does not mean you are lying.

In legal terms, a 'refugee' is someone who has had their claim for asylum accepted by the Home Office. In the 1951 United Nations Convention, a refugee is defined as a person who has a well-founded fear of being persecuted for reasons of race, religion, nationality, membership of a particular social group or political opinion. In order to be recognised as a refugee you have to convince the Home Office that you would be persecuted for one of these reasons if you went back to your country. This can be very hard to prove, even for someone who was a political prisoner and has been tortured by their government.

75% of claims for asylum are refused, sometimes because people can't provide enough evidence to prove their claims but often just because the system is stacked against them. Some people are detained on a 'fast track' where they never see the light of day from the moment they arrive and where they are not given time to even build a case. Some people are discriminated against because they are still traumatised by their experiences, for example we have known women who have been subject to sexual violence in their country and are unable to share the details of rape and assault with strangers so the Home Office has dismissed their stories. Some people are simply never given the chance to make a successful claim because their home country is on a list of so-called 'safe countries', including places where people are persecuted for their sexuality such as Nigeria or Jamaica, and other countries such as Sri Lanka which are known for political killings, violence against women and torture in police custody.

Being refused asylum does not mean that the claim was bogus, or that the person was lying. Sometimes the Home Office does come right out and accuse someone of "negative credibility", but more than 1 in 4 of all asylum refusals that go to appeal are overturned by a judge on the basis that the Home Office has made a mistake, and that the person should have been granted refugee status in the first place.

It also varies depending on the country in which you claim asylum. The UK only grants around 25% of claims but Switzerland and Finland grant a much higher 70%. In Ireland on the other hand it is 10% while in Greece it is less than 1%. The overall effect is something of a European asylum lottery.

The myth: Britain is the Number One destination for refugees.
Busted: The UK is not Number One in the world. It is not even Number One in Europe.

According to the 2009 UN Human Development Report, 214 million people are currently living outside their national borders – a figure that includes some 50 million 'illegal' migrants and 14 million refugees, and does not include the 26 million Internally Displaced Persons who remain inside their national borders and therefore are not classified as refugees.

There are around 195,500 refugees in the UK. That is just 1% of the total number of refugees in the world. Most people who flee their homes end up in their neighbouring country, and about 80% of the world's refugees are living in developing countries, often in camps. Africa and Asia between them host more than three quarters of the world's refugees. Europe looks after just 15%. As an example, over 490,000 refugees have fled the conflict in Democratic Republic of Congo, including about 15,000 in 2011. In that year, just 188 of them applied for asylum in the UK. Of those in Europe, there are higher rates in Germany and France than the UK, with most of the refugees in the West living in the USA.

The myth: Asylum seekers are responsible for mass immigration to the UK
Busted: Asylum seekers only make up 0.27% of the population

Refugees only make up a small amount of the total migrants in the UK. In 2011 the number of people who came to the UK and claimed asylum was just 3% of the total number of immigrants.

The most common countries of birth for foreign-born people in the UK are India, Poland, Pakistan, Ireland, Germany and the United States. The most common country of origin for foreign citizens are Poland, India, Ireland, Pakistan and the United States; whereas the most common countries of origin for refugees are places like Iran, Syria, Afghanistan and Eritrea. Asylum seekers from places like India are usually processed by detained "fast-track", so they are held in detention centres, are very rarely granted refugee status and are unable to appeal against the decision to remove them back to India.

In 2012, refugees and asylum seekers made up just 0.27% of the UK population.

The myth: Asylum seekers are given priority over other council tenants for housing
Busted: Asylum seekers do not get council housing

Asylum seekers are not allowed to apply for council houses. They do not go on the housing list. They might be housed by the Home Office in a bed and breakfast, often sleeping an entire family to one room with no facilities for cooking. These are not provided or paid for by the council. These are often places like empty hotels or B&Bs used for homeless people with drug or alcohol problems. Once people seeking asylum have been granted leave to remain in the UK they have the same rights as other citizens and can queue up on the council housing waiting list if they need to. They are not entitled to jump the queue any more than anyone else.

Who wins the war? Memories of the
Second World War in Burma

Eleanor Clarke with Lorna Stephenson

"Sometimes you can't believe it's happened! I don't ever get bored, because I can just switch off and think, 'Fancy me being there!' There's a wonderful Shan saying that mother used to say: If you take a long time to die, you live so many reincarnations. This is me. It's like a metamorphosis, every step is completely different".

Meeting Eleanor Clarke in her small flat in a Brighton tower block, you could not begin to imagine the incredible experiences she has had. Born Eleanor Gaudoin and brought up in colonial Burma, she had a 'silver spoon' childhood as the daughter of the Deputy Commissioner and a Shan princess. Eleanor left Burma for the UK by boat in 1958, when life in Burma, after years of civil war, had become increasingly difficult. Travelling alone with her young children, on arrival in the UK she found her husband

and they built a new life from nothing, living in poverty but, as Eleanor says, "we managed".

Here are her memories of the Second World War, which shattered the privileged upbringing she had enjoyed and turned her family's life upside down. After fleeing the palace, the family first hid from the Japanese in rural villages, then were kept under house arrest, before fleeing again when the Japanese began to lose the war. Eventually, after an arduous and dangerous journey which brought them close to death, they arrived at the American 101 base just as the war was drawing to a close.

I was born in Myitkyina, in the northern Kachin states of Burma, on the 25th July, 1933. My father was deputy commissioner there, before he was transferred to Mawlaik – a bigger town and a bigger position. We had a huge house with a tennis court served by butlers and gardeners, and lots of Indian servants who dressed in red turbans and white tunics. I was a child, so I was sent to the nursery during the evening dinners, but I remember tiptoeing into the dining room and seeing the table laid with bowls of chocolate. When the gong went my mother and older sisters would traipse down in their long dresses, my mother swishing with silk and wearing her lovely jewels.

My mother and father's marriage had caused a huge scandal. My father was from a mixed European and Indian background and was high up with the Frontier Service. He was married with eight children. My mother was just 20, and a Shan 'premier princess', with five ladies in waiting. They ran off together on horseback in 1920. My uncle wanted my father's life, and nothing less. He chased them on horseback and was going to shoot my mother for bringing shame on the family, she was already engaged to the Soapha of Hsipaw, but my father said, "You can shoot me first!". He was a brilliant man and returned to the service as the only person who could speak the local languages of Burma fluently. He even wrote the first Hakha-Chin dictionary, which is now in the Brighton Museum.

I was the youngest of seven children, the baby of the family, and I was brought up almost like an only child because of the difference in age between me and my siblings, who all attended boarding school. My early years were a child's paradise. My father was a guarantor for the Italian community in a town called Maymyo, and on one visit there I remember my father parking and I ran to the sweet and pastry shop down the road. I went in and declared, "I'm a Gaudoin!". Mr Angelo came running out and said, "Give her anything she wants!". I had snowballs. I didn't attend school, but spent all my time with my father, driving around with him in his car.

I think I became aware of the war when Singapore was attacked, I don't know what year that was, perhaps the beginning of 1942 because after Singapore it was Burma. My father said, and these are his words, "Singapore will never fall, it's impregnable!". My mother would reply in Shan, "It will, it's written in the Demyne", which is like an almanac, or book of prophesies. She was an intellectual, and she knew a lot about Buddhist scriptures. My father said "Bah!", he loved using that word, "Bah!". But then we were packing. We could have gone to India, my father had connections there. I remember the morning because we had the most magnificent brass bed, inlaid with mother of pearl, that I'd sleep in with my parents. The sun was shining on the bed that morning, it looked heavenly. We were all packed. But then my mother decided she didn't want to leave. That's when the whole trouble started.

Instead, we went back to Hsenwi to the old palace where my grandmother was. Suddenly one day they said, "You've got to evacuate now! Get out of Hsenwi!". I sat choosing which toys I wanted to bring, and what else to leave or take. I was left by myself to pack my things, the servants were all busy packing their belongings or items in the palace. My father was behaving as if he were going to the office or something, but it was terribly important that we didn't meet any Japanese on the way, they would have shot us all out of hand. We went to the south of the Namtu river which ran through the Hsenwi state. The bridge over it was a very strategic point during the war. There were hills surrounding it, beautiful hills, all you could see when you looked out of the window. We went down the river to where my uncle, the Soapha had already had thatch and bamboo houses built, for him and his family, a bit further in. We stayed in this little ferry hut, that used to be used by the ferryman who ferried passengers from one side of the Namtu to the other. It was a beautiful spot. My parents were eccentric, impractical people; my mother royal, brilliant and a bit mad. They decided to store food for the war, buying lots of cream crackers, condensed milk, and sugar. I'd spend all afternoon crumbling the crackers and adding the milk and sugar. It was lovely. But I was very badly bitten by fleas.

So we stayed in the little hut but we had to go up across the jungle to visit where my grandmother and uncle and his entourage were. It was quite dangerous really, I had to go on my own. I would cross a huge chasm on just a single tree trunk, with the monkeys chattering above up in the trees. Once a day we did that, for meals with my grandmother. My sisters Elaine and Evelyn were there, and a cousin of ours who was a Unnani princess - Unnan was part of Burma, but now is part of China again - who my mother had decided to bring to Hsenwi. Her grandmother also came once, and that was how I saw opium getting smoked. I went into this room and I remember the smell of the raw opium. They toasted it and she had a big pipe and was laying down on the bed. Her son's concubines were all kneeling, they rolled it into a little ball and then toasted it and put it in the pipe. I can still remember the clouds of opium smoke, I can still smell it.

I think at that point for children the war was very exciting. When I left my dolls behind and we were evacuated to this little hut, I remember the terrible petrol explosions, the black holes of smoke, because they wanted to destroy everything after the British left. Gasoline. But in a way there wasn't any fear. It was, "Things are going to change". My father stayed very calm when he was with me.

I used to swim everyday on that riverbank. It was a lovely place, there were lots of dragonflies and a little island in the middle. But the river used to be very discoloured because of all the bodies, reddish, because there was a lot of slaughter going on further up the river, but we still went swimming. I remember falling in one time, I was rescued by my uncle's secretary and his family who saw me and pulled me out. We all suffered malaria. It was awful, you'd be shivering and then you'd get very hot and have hallucinations. I remember seeing a grain of rice getting bigger and bigger and rolling down a hill to crush me.

One night, a whole lot of young Chinese soldiers came through. They were starving and stuffed themselves with raw rice in the kitchen. I heard later on there was about 100 of them, and even though I was a child I recognised they were still very young, teenagers. None of them escaped, they were slaughtered going across the river by the locals. We had a whole lot of refugees coming down from China.

At some point while we were there, someone asked about my brother, they said, "Where's Alec?", and the answer: "Well, he's still in Maymyo!" - "We should go and get him then!". He was about thirteen and the Second World War was rumbling on, and he was hundreds of miles away! My father went to get him, and I hid in the car and stowed away. Halfway down I said, "I'm here!". It was a memorable journey because of all the refugees, the roads were packed with them. We had to stop at a dark bungalow overnight because we could hardly move in the road with the refugees, they were clinging to the car. A lot of them were trying to walk to India. My brother had already left with a sister-in-law, to take a train. My father called the station master to get the train stopped and we found Alec in the middle of nowhere.

We returned to the house by the riverbank, but soon the family was on the move again to travel back through Hsenwi to go to Saiu. The journey was difficult, there were dead bodies, so many of them, all Chinese and all shot. It was the worst thing I have ever seen. My brother kept saying 'Look, some ill children'. It's funny, really, you have a shutter that comes down. You wonder how children survive the traumas of war... I remember one corpse very vividly for some reason. It was a Chinese man in khaki shorts and a singlet. He had been shot in the back of his head and he had a little bundle under his arm. That was more poignant. The car was actually bumping over the corpses. Sometimes when I wanted to speak English I did, and I did now. "Daddy," I remember asking, "Do the Japanese look like caterpillars?"

Every time the Japanese came round my father used to hide himself in a roll of matting so they wouldn't see. We had to hide until we had clearance. It was my ninth birthday when my father went to meet the Japanese officially. They were all sitting round a table and he had a guarantor who was an ex-colleague from the Burmese Frontier Service, who was very pro-Japanese. The Japanese distrusted my father, but his guarantor wrote and said my father wouldn't spy or do any subversive work.

My brother David used to drive these big Chinese trucks down from China, and he used to say nobody would think anything of, you know, stabbing the other driver. These trucks used to fall off the hairpin bends and nobody bothered to rescue anyone. They were dead anyway. He did that for a long time and then, at the age of 18, he joined the RAMC as an ambulance driver. What they did, they had put the last of the wounded onto the planes and then were to walk to India. He didn't make it. He got cholera, he caught it on the way and the group had to leave him behind. He was only 19. He was a true and kind person, David.

The Japanese officers who came to visit were always very courteous and gave all the family arm bands to identify them. My father wasn't allowed to go anywhere, like house arrest really. You had to keep a very, very low profile. My parents and uncle played bridge all day long. I had to go to the school which had been taken over by the Japanese. The Burmese headmaster was still there, he really disliked a new teacher, a young Japanese man, and he was very brave to show it! His young son had to go up on this water tank to sound the alarm for air raids. The air raids were strategic because the school had nothing between it and the bridge, just paddy fields. The bridge was bombed every day. Every day you could hear the heavy sound of the planes coming in. You could tell the difference with the American planes.

A headmaster in Hsenwi was a friend of my mother's, and for some reason he was taken away and badly tortured. They brought back his body and dumped it on the step, with all his arms and legs disjointed. He died about three days later. He must have been in agony because we didn't even have aspirin. If you needed an operation, it was done without anaesthetic. There was no medicine. Although I remember the Japanese used to go around and give everyone an anti-plague injection in the market, there used to be guards at the entrance and they wouldn't let people leave until they had had it. At school, they'd shut the gates and everyone had to have the injections and they'd spray you to get rid of germs. They were very health conscious like that.

At this time I was picked to dance at the concerts they sometimes had in Hsenwi, with classical music and the Thunder and Lightning waltz, I remember that. They had cherry blossoms falling over the orchestra. I was the child star, and was given a very bright pink kimono which I had to wear holding a doll and singing a song in Japanese about it. I was fluent in Japanese at the time. I can still remember the song, and it was sixty something years ago! An officer used to tell my mother, "I will take your daughter to Tokyo and make her a famous actress!". One day a low rank officer came and told my mother they wanted to take me to Kunglung to dance, because it was the northern command and they had a general there. My mother didn't want to let me go, Kunglung was very notorious and we heard they did all the torture there. But the teacher said, "You have no choice, madame," I can hear him saying that, "No choice".

It was all soldiers who saw the concerts, I think coming back from the front, along with local dignitaries they had invited. I didn't really notice, I was a real little show off and loved the singing and dancing. I was in my element. It was about 60 miles to Kunglung and on the way we stopped at a beautiful waterfall with a pool which we bathed in, I remember beautiful dragonflies all around. We stopped for a meal and I remember one of the Japanese trying to roast an egg in the fires embers. It was raw when he cracked it but he ate it anyway. At Kunglung, we did a couple of shows, I'm not sure how many. They had monkeys in cages. I was called into the general's office. He only had one eye. He was a very powerful man, after all he was general of the northern command and he put people to death, tortured them, everything. He put me on his lap and the extraordinary thing was that his room was full of little bottles of sweets.

The war was coming to an end and the Japanese saw the writing on the wall and said "Go!". That was when the Americans bombed the whole town with the 'scorcher policy'. The old palace took three days to burn down. There was no one there, the Japanese had gone as well, so they bombed everything that was worth bombing. It took days and days.

We left Hsenwi for a little village called Denyet. My father would get out a cricket bat and play cricket with my brother. When we were there a very elite Japanese corps, who spoke good English and were very well educated, would come to see us. Whenever there was a raid they'd go and stand outside in white silk. My mother would say, "Please come in!", and they'd say, "It's alright, you've got a radio to keep in touch with the British haven't you?". She was a nervous wreck and at night I'd sleep in the trenches with her. It was oozing with damp, with earthworms coming out. Sometimes we'd have a little fire so it wouldn't be too cold, but I have always had arthritis and I had terrible aches and pains.

They thought we were spies, they came to my father and they kept saying, You've got a radio and he kept saying, "No! We haven't got a radio!". My father decided to keep a cow and built a cow shed, but any new building would draw bombing, mercifully they missed the target! No one would accept money at the time, because of inflation and all the money being printed, but the tribes would accept men's clothing. My brother was down to one pair of pants and one pair of pantaloons. I remember one day he was having his pantaloons washed and was wearing my mother's skirt and I giggled. My mother gave me a jolly good hiding for that! He'd had to give up everything for rice and things. My father had a big lump of opium and that was handy, we could exchange that for food. Most of the Chinese smoked opium.

When we were in Denyet the Americans were coming in and air lifting all the Sopalls and the royalty, when the war was still going on. But we were sort of left out of that, they were in touch with the rest of the family but not us. So one day we moved from there to another village which was much deeper in the jungle. There were no roads or anything and there were no Japanese, they wouldn't dare to come because the war was going badly for them. They couldn't risk ambushes, and the Americans were penetrating from the north. Tragic things happened at this time. When the Americans took villages and then retreated, the Japanese would come back and slaughter everyone in a complete massacre. There was terrible torture, someone says they had boiled his wife. It was terrible, one day the Americans were there and they thought they were safe, and then what happens?

I think, who loses the war? I've heard some terrible stories of things done by the allied troops, by the people who did them. There was a young lieutenant, our neighbour, who said they kept Japanese soldiers alive even though they were horribly burned with napalm to get confessions out of them. Who loses the war?

One day in the jungle we went to sit and have something to eat. A runner came, a Shan who had no shirt or nothing, and he was covered in sweat and very frightened. He said, "You must come with me, you must come, they've got your father and your brother". They had gone to find my uncle and find out what he was planning to do. He had already been airlifted by the Americans. It was on their way back that they were ambushed, by a group of Japanese, who included my old teacher. He had been returning to the village when some Kachin people came to him and said "You mustn't go that way, the Japanese!", but he was obstinate and didn't listen, then of course came across this Japanese party. They were arrested at bayonet point. The Japanese, including the intelligence corps who had visited us, were all staying in the caves on the other side of the town. We landed up there, but first were taken to the headquarters near to the caves.

They sent Indian National soldiers to get us, because it was too dangerous for the Japanese in the jungle at that point. They sent a truck but we had to walk miles and miles to where they were. Just through honour we could have escaped but they already had my father and brother. If they were with us we would have escaped. I remember my teacher was there for some reason and I even sat on his lap! He had just stopped my brother being executed. It was dark by the time we got to the truck. We hadn't had anything to eat that day, and they gave me a packet of biscuits with the little bit of icing on top. So they took us to the headquarters, on the other side of Hsenwi, and they had caves there as well.

They were very suave and spoke wonderful English. We were all interrogated first, and I sat in the room with the servants to interpret for them and my sister, as I was the only one who spoke fluent Japanese apart from my brother, who was already in custody. They were asking about the attack on the Japanese group, were we involved in that, were we involved with my uncle? They couldn't believe that we had been left behind to face the music. There was a big oil drum and we were told someone had been boiled alive there, a few days before, to intimidate us. They could have shot us all, but I think they felt quite sorry for us in a way.

Then they took us to this island with this Japanese camp commander, Captain Horicta. He was a very good man, a very gentle sort of man and he spoke English quite well. Without him, we wouldn't be alive today. I don't know where it was exactly, this little island. There were lots of other people there who had been arrested, high-ranking people, and I remember roaming around it to go and see people. We were built a very leaky hut and my family would play games in the evening and sing. We were there for a month or two.

One day, Captain Horicta called us: "I have been ordered to shoot all of you, but I can't do it."

He said, "You must escape tonight, but if you meet any Japanese patrols, you won't survive. They have nothing to lose and you'll be killed". He had been ordered, now the war was ending, to take us to Thailand or execute us. By now the Japanese had scattered, each man for himself – they were even disguising themselves as trees! They had nothing to lose, and were fanatical, they didn't want to surrender.

So we escaped from the camp, starting off in a cart but then we walked. It must have been April, because at one point we were crossing a river and they said it's Burmese New Year. We went to a village nearby. One day, we had left the village for the day and came back to find all our clothes had been bayoneted. Had we been there, I wouldn't be here now, we were very close to death. The same day, my maid and I went to visit an aunt in another house, and when we came back there was nobody there! A young cowherd was seated on a buffalo playing the flute, and I asked, "Where have all the people gone?". He said, "That way", pointing to the jungle. So we went, and found my mother, she hadn't waited for me! She had a Burmese saying, "If the world is on fire, you even put your child down as a stepping stone!".

By now I think my father and Uncle Saoyip had made their way to the American 101. I never asked my father what their journey was like, but they made it. We decided we would go and join them. One village we stayed at, we woke in the morning and everyone had left because we were leading the Japanese to them. We were dangerous to have around. At another village, high up in the hills, they had never seen anyone Japanese in their lives, nor seen the British, so when they saw us they ran. They thought that we were Japanese. It was beautiful up there in the mountains, very cold and the people wore tribal costume and spoke Shan. They grew tea in beautiful terraces, and had wonderful wild raspberries. The houses there were all made of wood and the pigs were kept beneath them – when you went to the toilet, you had to take a stick with you to beat the pigs away. The opium came in handy for exchanging, they didn't know what currency was anyway. I can't remember how long we stayed there. We left, making our way out towards the Americans.

We walked 23 miles one day to the American camp. There was about thirty of us: my Uncle Saoyip's party, my mother, my two sisters and brother and all our servants, just the women and children because my father had gone already. Everyone was struggling, each for their own. You just kept walking in one direction and if you saw someone ahead, you followed them. I think we did stop for a meal that day, a curry, near a stream. But there was a lot of fear. But you know, it's funny because when you are in that state you cut off. You wonder how people survive the Holocaust, terrible concentration camps... Our experience was nothing compared to that, just close to death that's about it. You never thought "I'm close to death", you just switch off and keep walking.

When we got to the 101 camp, I arrived with my mother. To be honest, I can't remember what emotions I had. The first thing the Americans asked when we got there was, "What would you like to eat?". I answered, "Bacon and eggs, please!". I got it, tinned bacon and powdered egg, scrambled, and I loved it!

Bienvenue à Calais

Lorna Stephenson

"The end of the right to asylum is at the core of the
criminalisation of movement from one country to
another, and at the strategic centre of the rejection
of foreigners. It not only has a democratic impact,
through the number of applications refused, but also
an immediate symbolic effect through the refusal of
the minimum of humanity to which each human being
is entitled....This leads to the identification and
sidelining of part of the world population, as
'remains', 'waste', 'surplus', qualified merely as
undesirables. It also leads to arbitrary insults and
contempt, and eventually to the right to shoot, to
injure or kill, which some police feel entitled to
exercise at borders. Applied to all those 'without', the
word undesirable refers to this vacuum, this roaming
in time and space. So, at the very moment when the
word appears as our shared destiny, indifference
becomes policy, criminalising universal solidarity
towards those who, formerly considered refugees,
are today refused all rights."
Michel Agier, anthropologist[1]

---

1   Agier, Michel. 'Exiles, refugees, displaced people, rejected
    applicants... Towards a world without asylum?' In: *Atlas of Migration
    In Europe*. p.19 Migreurop, 2013

Escaping the Syrian civil war, those who fled to
Europe no doubt expected more from the continent
that prides itself on its respect for human rights. In
Calais the bleak sight of the wind-battered tents on
muddy ground, known as the 'Syrian Camp',
illustrates the chasm between that hope and reality.
When groups of Syrian refugees began arriving in
late 2013, many reacted to their reception in Calais
with shock and indignation, staging a protest on the
footbridge of the port and camping defiantly next to
the roads leading to it. Months later, as the worst
winter in twenty years slowly morphed into spring,
the camp remained. The Syrians had been joined by
other nationalities – the numbers swelled to well over
a hundred - but the winds and rain seemed to have
driven out the desire to agitate. Being Syrian, they
had learned, means very little in Calais, just as
refugees from Sudan, Eritrea, Afghanistan, Iran and
many other unstable or repressive states had found
before them.

In Calais, you are simply an 'illegal immigrant',
and the consequences of that are dire. The border
zone, where France ends and is separated from the
UK by just 26 miles of the Channel, is a hub where
ruthless EU immigration policies play out daily, on
the pavements and in the parks, in squats and on the
sand dunes. Juxtaposed border control agreements
mean the UK Border Force is stationed in Calais port,
while the French forces police the town mercilessly.

Much media attention, particularly from
conservative publications, on the transient population
of migrants in Calais has also fixed on this narrative
of 'illegal immigrants', portraying them as
opportunistic criminals waiting to storm the border.

Just this year, the *Daily Mail* has claimed, 'Hundreds of illegal immigrants armed with knives and crowbars swarm round Calais trucks heading for Britain', and 'Up to 15,000 immigrants sneak into Britain through Calais every year'. The narrative is a fallacy and a denial; of the basic humanity of those deemed 'undesirable' and criminalised, of the mistreatment they suffer at the hands of the authorities, and finally of the political decisions which have created and perpetuated the crisis.

As the Syrians found, the living conditions in Calais are harsh for undocumented migrants, the number of whom fluctuates between around 300-500 at any one time. Homeless and with no money or recourse to public assistance, people survive living in tents and shelters made from scrap materials and tarpaulins. Others live in the open air, under railway bridges or hidden in bushes. Blankets, sleeping bags and clothing, which are distributed once a fortnight from a local church, are always in short supply. There are no sanitary facilities and little food. A French association, Salam, distributes one meal a day at a concrete compound near the port, under the watchful eyes of police who park to observe from the other side of the high, barbed wire-topped fences. In winter the town is battered by bitterly cold sea winds, compounding the health problems picked up by many on their journeys and making recovery from injury slow. Small fires provide the only warmth, but even firewood is hard to come by. The realities of Calais make the desire to cross to the UK, for those who aim to do so, ever more desperate and urgent.

The presence of migrants at the Channel ports has been a contentious issue for more than ten years, but political discussion has taken the form of a blame game rather than acknowledging that the issue is an acute humanitarian crisis. Just as when the British and French authorities forced the Red Cross-run refugee camp at Sangatte to close in 2002, the debate among politicians today centres on whether the 'immigration problem' in Calais is the responsibility of the French politicians on whose soil the drama is unfolding – or the British, whose maritime border is the wall behind which the migrants are caught.

As French politicians are quick to point out, the problem occurs because the UK is not part of the Schengen Agreement, which allows the free movement of citizens between EU countries. Maintaining autonomy to regulate its own borders, the UK has done so with relish. It now boasts one of the tightest border regimes in the world. Millions have been pumped into installing technology on the UK-France border in particular, with immigration officers using X-ray scanners and body heat, heartbeat and carbon dioxide sensors as just part of a matrix of high-tech security equipment that aims to make the border impassable for irregular migrants.

One effect of the new technology has been to push clandestine travellers to take even deadlier risks. To evade CO2 monitors, some people resort to holding plastic bags over their heads. Others risk freezing to death. One Afghan teenager I spoke to in Calais had a fractured shoulder and was deeply afraid of the 'mafia' whom he had already paid to smuggle him into trucks. He spoke only a few words of English, but tried to explain the fears keeping him awake at night: *'Cold truck, cold truck'*, he said, rubbing his arms. It transpired the smugglers worked on a 'ten chances' model. If you have still been unsuccessful after nine attempts in ordinary freight lorries, you must go in a refrigerated one. Deaths in refrigerated lorries, from hypothermia and suffocation, are well-documented. For the terrified 15-year-old, alone in Calais, this was being presented as the only option.

The desperate living conditions and the danger of any attempted onward journey are just part of what makes the lives of migrants here so tough. For years, a combination of the police forces which patrol Calais, most notably the immigration police, the PAF (*Police Aux Frontieres*), and the anti-riot squads, the CRS (*Compagnies Républicaines de Sécurité*), have carried out a sustained campaign of ID checks and arrests, continuous raids and closures of living spaces, and other actions on those 'sans papiers'. Reports of police violence against migrants are commonplace.

     Solidarity activists with Calais Migrant Solidarity, a grass-roots initiative which is part of the radical Europe-wide No Borders movement, have been monitoring the police repression in Calais since the camp clearances in 2009. The clearance of the mainly Afghan camps was a huge operation which involved several hundred riot police, who detained over 200 people of whom around half were minors. The camp was then bulldozed. Since then reports of mistreatment have continued. As one CMS activist put it, "A very macho, racist, violent culture pervades the police, particularly the border police and the riot police. It often feels like it is a game for them. The police's job is to catch migrants and this plays out like a witch hunt. The police will often high five each other during raids, make racist and degrading comments, referring to people as animals, or bark at people like they are dogs. People often say they are treated worse than animals".

In 2012, campaigners including CMS along with 23 other refugee and migrant organisations, scored a small coup when they presented evidence of police abuse to Dominique Baudis, France's Defender of Rights. Baudis instigated an investigation which concluded with a damning report on policing in the town. For migrants and on-the-ground activists it was nothing short of stating the obvious, but nevertheless it caused some ripples in the French parliament.

The accusations in his report amounted to an entrenched culture of harassment, and stressed that such actions deprived people of their rights and should stop. The harassment specified included ID controls based on racial profiling that take place day and night, including those places where migrants go to get handouts of food or other aid. It described repeated arrests, sometimes inflicted on the same person more than once in a day (those not detained for long face a tiring two-hour walk back from the detention centre, which is incongruently located in a large commercial complex outside of the city). The report documented police tactics of raiding sleeping places, seemingly purely to incite fear and "humiliate" migrants, and the police were further criticised for their evictions of shelters, during which they not only destroyed someone's living space but also their personal belongings, clothes and essential survival items like blankets and sleeping bags.

Unfortunately, but predictably, the report had little impact. For those of us on the ground, for some time it appeared the police took a more hands-off approach to migrants in public, while the Ministry of the Interior stalled its response long enough that when it eventually came - months later – the dust had already settled. The response was a complete denial, with the Interior Minister stating: "The points set out in your decision are based essentially on declarations made by representatives of associations, which quote non-verifiable statements concerning events which took place some time ago, and which cannot be supported by any objective facts today."

Excessive police action against migrants has tended to occur in waves but in the year since Baudis' report there seems to have been a shift of policy regarding squats and other places where migrants find essential shelter. Many old warehouses and other abandoned premises previously used as squats have been cleared. The Mayor of Calais, Natasha Bouchart, has been playing the anti-migrant card for months in the run up to the mayoral elections. Along with ordering a clampdown on migrants finding shelter in buildings through repeated rounds of evictions which campaigners say are illegal (under French law a court process should be followed if the building has been inhabited for longer than 48 hours), she has encouraged Calais residents to report all suspicious behaviour – such as looking at empty buildings - to a special phone line. As the deputy mayor, Phillipe Mignonet, has said, "maintaining a certain level of pressure on migrants" is crucial as "we want them to send a message back that it's useless to come to Calais". The realities of life for those like the Iranians I met, who held battered photographs of themselves at banned demonstrations against the regime in their pockets, are ignored.

Beyond the miserable living conditions and constant fear of police, the undocumented people in Calais face another considerable threat: the Dublin Regulation. This piece of legislation, enacted across the European Union, states that the first Member State where an asylum seeker appears is responsible for that person's claim. Calais is one place where the ghost of 'Dublin' haunts irregular migrants, as many have previously lodged asylum claims in other countries or have at least been fingerprinted there. Their biometric data might have been forcefully taken on arrest or control in previous countries, such as Greece or Italy, and then stored on the central database, EURODAC.   The stated political objective of the regulation is "to avoid asylum seekers from being sent from one country to another, and also to prevent abuse of the system by the submission of several applications for asylum by one person."[2] What this means in practice is that people whose asylum claim has been rejected in one place are denied the opportunity to apply elsewhere. The different refugee recognition rates in different states mean asylum seekers face a sort of 'asylum lottery'.
       If an asylum seeker is detained in another

---

2   Europa, 'Dublin II Regulation', accessed 29/04/2014 at:
    http://europa.eu/legislation_summaries/justice_freedom_security/fre
    e_movement_of_persons_asylum_immigration/l33153_en.htm

state, they can be sent back to the country where their prints were taken or their initial claim lodged, causing a distressing and pointless boomerang effect of deportation and repeated journeys. As a report by the European Council on Refugees and Exiles found in 2008, "All too often, a Dublin transfer [deportation] guarantees that asylum applications will *not* be meaningfully examined".[3] The statelessness that results forces people into increasingly precarious situations and destitution. As journalist Matthew Carr notes, "Within Europe, tens of thousands of asylum seekers have been trapped in bureaucratic limbo, in some cases for years, unable to become part of European or any other society."[4]

This certainly holds true in Calais. For many, the UK is a last resort, having had their claim turned down elsewhere. Dublin forces them to travel clandestinely and to remain underground. For these people, the UK's pull is not because it's seen as an asylum seeker's utopia - as some British politicians claim - but because it's the final chance, the end of the line. There are also many more people who stay without the intention to cross to the UK. The destitution and legal dead ends they've met have given them few options, and in Calais – for all the hardships – there is, at the very least, some sort of community.

---

3   ECRE, 2008, 'Sharing Responsibility for Refugee Protection in Europe: Dublin Reconsidered'. Accessed at: http://www.ecre.org/topics/areas-of-work/protection-in-europe/134.html
4   Carr, M, 2012, 'The Trouble with Fortress Europe', *Open Democracy*: http://www.opendemocracy.net/matthew-carr/trouble-with-fortress-europe

In Limbo in Europe: Osman

While in Calais, I spoke with Osman, a refugee from Sudan. His story illustrates how the broken EU asylum system - and the Dublin Regulation in particular - can throw a person's life into turmoil, and force them to spend years living in the shadows of society.

Would you like to introduce yourself?

My name is Osman, I come from Sudan and I am 33 years old. I left my area 13 years ago. I have been in Europe more than 8 years and I'm still here, in Calais.

What made you decide to leave your home?

When I left my country, there was big war in my area, with government and opposition groups. Some groups were helping the government to attack civilians. That's why a lot of people died in my country, more than 400 people were killed this way, and 2.7 million ran from the country. I left my area then I spent three years in the capital, then I had problems with the government there - that's why I left the whole country and am now here in Europe.

Where did you go when you first left Sudan?

When I first left, I went to Syria, then a few days after to Lebanon. I was three years in Lebanon, after Lebanon I went back to Syria and then to Turkey. I

was there five months, after that I travelled to
Greece.

*Can you explain how you tried to seek asylum from
Lebanon?*

I claimed asylum in Lebanon at the Australian
Embassy in Beirut. They sent all my files to Jordan,
and from there they were sent to Australia. I was in
Lebanon for one year and after that I got rejected. At
that time Lebanon had a big problem with the Syrian
government, so that's why they sent me to Europe.
It's near to Europe, Lebanon. They told me Australia
is far away and there are very racist people... At that
time I didn't know where my family was and I am not
married, I am single, so I did not appeal, and decided
I was going to try to come to Europe.

*So it was only after trying to claim asylum from the
Middle East that you decided to come to Europe?*

Yes. After that I came to Greece. I was not able to
claim asylum in Greece. I was there for one year,
after that I went to France. I did not claim asylum but
I tried to cross to the UK, but I didn't have any
chance because at that time there was a lot of snow
and control is very difficult here in Calais. That's why
I went back to Switzerland. I claimed asylum in
Switzerland at that time.

*When you were claiming asylum in Switzerland, how
was your living situation?*

The first time I claimed, there was a centre. It's like detention where you can stay. A lot of people, for one week sometimes or two weeks. From there you get transferred to another place, you get an interview. From there they give you somewhere where you can stay, two people in a room, and after then you can maybe get a single house in a town. That's why after six months I got a house in the town. I was there two years and a half. But then I got a negative decision from there. I got two letters from the administration and they didn't give me any chance to answer or appeal. That's why I feel angry, that's why I moved from Switzerland to Norway. I claimed asylum in Norway.

How long were you in Norway?

The first time it was six months, the second time another six months, so one year. Two times in Norway.

And they also refused your claim? What happened then?

Yeah, they refused the claim. The first time they said, "You do not have fingerprints in any country in the European Union, but you have claimed asylum in Switzerland, maybe we can take you back there". That's why they took me back to Switzerland, but they shoot me [deported me] from there, saying, "We were not in Europe, that's why we don't agree to have you in Switzerland". So then I went to Belgium to claim asylum. In Belgium, they found my fingerprint in Norway and the Norway people said,

"No, we sent this man to Switzerland". So that's why I didn't get any interview, instead they sent me to Switzerland again. When I got there they called the immigration police from the immigration centre and they took me to prison, for one year. Just like that! After that, they released me from prison and said: "You have to leave the country". That's why I packed and left for Belgium. The same day they put me in prison and I had another three months in prison. At that point I crossed from Ostend to UK, where the police again caught me and put me in prison for one week, then sent me back to Belgium.

So you have been put in detention before they have asked you about your asylum claim or why you are there?

Yes! First thing! That's why I say it's like a business for these people. Same with the people working in immigration and people working in administrations of human rights, they are doing business. They don't want to try to help people who have problems, or work out who has a problem or who doesn't. That's why it's bad - they're making mistakes with people. I claimed asylum two times in Belgium and after that I claimed two times in UK, and I claimed asylum in Holland, Luxembourg, in France too. I was also in police stations in Germany for one week, in Sweden one week, and in Denmark one week, but I couldn't claim asylum there.

So these are places you went to, but they didn't give you a chance to make your case?

Yes, I travelled there and when the police catch you they put you in prison for one week. Maybe they'll find your fingerprint and send you somewhere else. If they don't find your fingerprint, maybe they'll say to you, "You must make an asylum claim or move out of the country". Still now, out of all of the European Union, no countries have really listened to my problems. No country has done an interview to ask me why I came to Europe. Never, never, never! They don't give me any chance, in any country. More than eight years now, I am in Europe. It's all the same, no chance. There's a lot of people here in Calais in the same situation. All these people, no house, no money, nothing. That is something bad! The human rights officials don't want to admit there is a problem.

Could you describe what your life is like here in Calais?

Yeah, my life is dead now. I don't have a life. More than nine months now I have stayed here in Calais. I don't get money, any house. Like this winter - how can you stay in a squat? Even if you get a squat the police won't leave you alone. If you stay in the jungle [camps] and try to make a fire, the police won't leave you. What can you do in the winter? Even people here in Calais are racist people. They won't give you any food. Even at the association at Salam, they give you some food to eat but they have stopped the lunch, you can't get food in the day or breakfast, you can only take dinner. I don't understand why they are doing that. The majority of the people here in Calais are horrible.

The problems are because of Dublin, you have fingerprint in Italy or somewhere. Of the 400 people in Calais, the majority is like that. That's why I say the people working in human rights are doing something bad, making mistakes. They see your face, give you negative, they just don't care. It's not a thousand people, not ten thousand people, not a million. This is four hundred or five hundred in Calais. You have to give them some country to finish. All these people in Europe become a criminal and have no life. A lot of people from different countries are all here, they have toured all of Europe for a lot of years. That's no good. How can you think of tomorrow? You forget the big picture. A lot of people are in prison, a lot of people have no life, a lot of people are deported to other countries. You don't know about tomorrow, what will happen.

What has been your experience of the police here?

The Police Nationale are not so bad, but immigration police are bullies. They do a lot of bad things. I don't think people realise what they do. There should be an investigation into the immigration police, and what they do to people.

What are your hopes for your future?

For me, I hope someone opens my file. Anywhere, I don't know. Anywhere. I can then rejoin my life once more. When my country is OK and they change the government, I'll go back to live my life in my country. All Sudanese people who left - if they now have papers or not - all people will go back when it changes to continue life there. All immigrant people in Calais, this is not life. It's not your last life in the world, or your last life in Europe, so you must try to do something or change something. Try to think about tomorrow and today. Yesterday is finished. European people should try to do something, make an investigation, look at the big picture, look at the problems. Try to change something.

"Everything Is Different to What I Thought Before." Reflections on Recovery from PTSD

Husnu Koluman with Meriel Beattie

Husnu Koluman, a Kurdish refugee from Turkey, shares his experience of post-traumatic stress disorder and explains how it has shaped his views on politics and the asylum system.

For a long time, eight or nine years, I didn't know I had post-traumatic stress. I think I first heard about it in the UK. I didn't know how it affected people. That's the big problem: people don't realise they have it, and that it's a serious condition. They call it 'post-traumatic stress', but it's more than stress, so maybe there should be a name change to make it stronger-sounding. Everything has changed in your brain and it's scary: you don't want to go out, you're scared of other people.

PTSD had an impact on all aspects of my life. I didn't get involved in social life. I was staying at home, studying, feeling sometimes angry, panicky, nervous. One day I went to college to read something and I don't quite know how it happened, but when I came to college I felt very scared and very uncomfortable. I was somewhere really deep.

Physical tasks, such as cleaning your house or cleaning your room, having a daily routine – you've lost interest in things like that. You don't do it, because of the stress and the trauma. The problem is your brain gets stuck in history. You don't think – OK, I'm here now, I'm all right, today I need to do this, or that. Always you're still analysing history: why did this happen? And this? This? And this?

I remember receiving my letter from the Home Office giving me British citizenship. It looked like a certificate but I didn't trust it. You don't realise that your brain map has changed. Your brain is thinking negative, negative, negative – because you have got used to that - even if it's something positive. It's very complicated but the most important thing you have to realise is, is this real? Or not? Your fear, your life. You have to realise where you are.

Several difficult events caused and exacerbated my post-traumatic stress. My history with the Home Office started in 1999 when I left Turkey and fled to Germany. When the German authorities refused my case I came to the UK. The UK said, "Sorry – you came from Germany". They sent me back to Germany and from there I was deported back to Turkey. There was torture, many things happened. Then I came back to the UK. I had been in prison in Germany for three months, for no reason. They said I didn't have documents. At the same time, I was diagnosed with diabetes and told I needed injections. Four, five problems all came together at once.

I think I understand the cause of my PTSD. It happened because the key was not in my hands – it was in someone else's. They could do what they wanted. That was the problem. You need to get the key into your own hands. You need to be able to arrange your life how you want it. The other problem was to learn how to stay calm and strong and to accept the circumstances – whatever they might be, it doesn't matter. If you don't you get angry, and that doesn't help. Anger is human nature, but it's a very negative force.

Despite my suffering, the process of getting help was a slow one. After eight or nine years, I recognised that this was a negative feeling and not a positive force. I felt anger but I couldn't get anywhere. Revenge is not good – you simply waste your time. After many years of more and more suffering you say, "OK, I'm fed up with this – so much has happened to me, but where's the solution?". You can't cope like that – you need to get out. You want to change your life to something new, better. That's the main thing. You don't want that other, dark life. You need to build a light life – if you can. Of course it's not easy though, I could see that.

Eventually I asked the GP. The process started like that. The GP gave me tablets and referred me to a psychologist. The GP himself doesn't have direct experience. They can say, "You have post-traumatic stress", and they can give you medication. But this medication is not a solution. It might make you feel better, like a painkiller, or help you sleep a bit better, but the problem will still be there. You need to look at the heart of the problem. I wasn't calm. I wasn't strong in the whole circumstances. I had problems as a child – I was a very shy child, worried, different. When I came here too, I felt shy, I didn't do anything.

Crucial to my recovery was speaking to the psychologist, and doing my own reading and research to understand what was going on in my brain. I spoke with a psychologist every week for eight or nine months. When you are shy and you have spent many years keeping things inside, it makes you a completely different person, in a negative way. I think the most helpful thing was that I was able to take what was inside me out. To talk. To find time to do something about it. When you have problems you have to take action, whether you are successful or not, to try to find a solution to what is wrong with you.

The psychologist just said, you need to become strong. Don't worry about what happened. It's passed, everything will go away. But the most important thing is you. When you start talking, your body is able to relax. You talk, you talk, it comes out. But if you don't bring it out, it stays inside for the rest of your life. You have to realise you need help. You have to make yourself conscious that you have a problem, and you need to understand that to find a solution will take time. There is no easy door. You may not find a solution tomorrow, or even next year. It may take many, many years. The brain is a very sensitive organ. When it's damaged, it can take many years to repair.

I think the real medication is in the understanding of the condition – not the doctor, not the psychologist. Because you go in deep to find the reality. You need to take the opportunity to think deeply about what exactly your problem is. When you find your problem, it's easier to find the solution. Thinking, how you think, is the most important thing. Logical thinking, deep thinking: what is reality, and what is not reality? What is real? What is false? Because many people with post-traumatic stress hold onto things which are false. They believe what they want to believe. I did this too.

You learn many things during this process, then you implement them slowly. Step by step is important. I made the mistake of trying to go fast. Here in Brighton I was trying to study, trying to deal with the Home Office, dealing with medication, and dealing with financial problems because at that time the Home Office stopped my payments. It was £37, but they stopped it. I was having to write letters and go back to have appointments with them every two months. I was also not healthy – it was difficult to deal with it all. It brings a lot of stress, a lot of pressure, and slowly, slowly, you collapse.

The solution is your own: how you think, how you are doing in your daily life. You need to learn not to follow empty things. Now I live better. In the morning I get up, make breakfast, I go out, I look around, I read, write, and manage myself in a positive way. Before I was scared to go out, I was scared of people and I would stay home, feeling sadness or anger. Now it's different – I manage my day slowly, not in a hurry and it's much more healthy. I don't worry much or have much stress or anxiety. My world has slowly changed. Everything is different to what I thought before. Everything becomes more positive, more acceptable.

Being active and getting out is so important. That's why, maybe four, five months ago, I was walking along the street and I saw a sign about hot yoga. I thought maybe it's helpful. I needed physical exercise because for many years the whole of my body felt infected with stress. It's not just your brain – your muscles are tight and you have to learn how to relax. And it was good because as you sweat you lose some of what's inside. You become more logical, because doing yoga your brain is concentrating on quite difficult physical exercises. The organisers said that it was good for stress, depression and anxiety, and it was very helpful. I would recommend it to many people.

I would say that I have got better in the last six to eight months. It's new, brand new. Every day, I still have problems but I know what I have to do to deal with them.

* * *

I've met many other refugees on my journey who had some kind of problem, they were suffering in some way. Many of them would take alcohol, drugs, something like that. I think language is so important. The government should make a law that people who come here have to learn the language. There's no question about this: it's reality. Language is the most important thing – you need to express yourself and you need to understand what is going on around you in the place where you are now living. If you don't understand that, then in your head you are still living in Turkey or whatever country you came from.

Many people who are in London and still cannot speak English have trauma, stress, or other mental health problems. They are suffering, but they cannot understand what's going on or how to ask for help, and they might not even know that they are suffering. It's difficult to get an interpreter because there have been government cuts. If you don't have English you can't even go to the GP. The GP isn't the whole solution, but he can at least help with tablets to help you sleep. You don't just need to be able to talk, you need to be able to read a lot of things and use the internet. I found many, many interesting pieces of information on the internet in scientific journals. It's not easy – but if you don't learn English, you'll never, ever be able to help yourself.

The other thing that makes things very difficult for refugees and asylum seekers is the Home Office, and the people working there. They didn't live in another country, they didn't suffer or have pay the same kind of price. It's difficult for them to understand the human reality. You might be afraid, have problems with your health or be anxious. There are many things the people in the office might not understand. It is easy to say, "Come to Croydon", but where do you get money, or a psychologist's statement, or something to eat, or drink. Every week they would say to me, "Come to Croydon", but what was my psychological state? How was I getting food? Or money? It's too easy for them to say to someone, "OK – refuse". Maybe they need to be shown what is reality, what are the real problems, and what might be the solutions.

Of course it's difficult to solve, but as a person, you have to fight. You have to feel you can say, "Look, I don't think you really understand my reality, you don't understand my situation". You have to have that right, but it's hard to make them understand. They have not felt those pressures and I think that they are doing many cases wrong. But the Home Office is very difficult to change. All change is difficult and, in fact, only experience really changes you. If you can fight for your rights maybe you have a chance.

* * *

Now, I am fascinated by neuroscience and its impact on society. I would like to know many things. I'm interested to know how do you find the best brain to run the justice system? What is the best brain to run the economy? And peace is so important too. If you don't have peace there will always be problems with something. Peace, the economy and justice.

Neurology plays a big part. I think people need to understand that the people who are managing justice or the economy, they come from rich families, they don't know what is going on. David Cameron comes from a rich family. He doesn't understand what it is to be poor, what it is to suffer.

Some people have pain – but you don't really understand completely unless you have felt that pain too. When you've never suffered, you think everything is OK. You think that the people that are suffering are not behaving in the right way. They seem to be doing stupid things and you make negative comments about them – but you're wrong.

You don't really understand them or why they are doing this, why they are thinking in this way. I think the people who make the best economists, the best peace-brokers, the best people for the justice system, are people who have suffered first. Seeing, observing, is not enough. You don't completely understand it, or feel it. You don't know the deep reality. And in my opinion, people need to understand that and only then get power. Not just rich families who move from one big building to another, enjoy life, talk, and say, "I want to make the economy better". Real life is not like that.

The Impact of Trauma – Individual, Society, Recovery and Growth.

Husnu Koluman interviews psychologist and trauma expert Shawn Katz, Ph.D.

Shawn Katz is a Chartered and Registered Counselling Psychologist, Integrative Psychotherapist, and EMDR Consultant. He works in an Integrative way, and specialises in the assessment and treatment of trauma and complex trauma.

Husnu Koluman: First of all I would like to thank you very much for your invitation. What changes in the brain with someone who has post-traumatic stress disorder (PTSD)?

Shawn Katz: There are parts of the brain that are responsible for determining and evaluating danger and threat. So the part of the brain that is determining whether something is threatening or not is over-active. Think in terms of a smoke alarm: It's a machine that determines smoke, but it's not going to make a difference whether there's a big fire going on, or it's just burnt toast. When you have post-traumatic stress, your brain's determining every signal, misinterpreting it, as a real fire – instead of burnt toast. This is the more emotional part of your brain. The thinking part of your brain, the cortex, the newer part, goes offline. So when you've had trauma, the part of your brain that gets to think clearly is kind of switched off. You are going to interpret things that are not in and of themselves threatening, as threatening. Some of that's going to be reminders – it could be a smell, a sound, a face, a time of day – any trigger that you have that is going to remind you of your trauma is going to activate the smoke alarm as being threatening.

HK: But does the human brain have the capability to say, "OK, this is not dangerous", and switch off the alarm?

SK: Sure, but it might take a lot of practice, training and mindfulness to learn how to reprogram yourself. You've had flashbacks? So you're talking about the experience of perceiving something that's not there. So what happens? How do you pull yourself back? Well if you think of memory there's a part of your brain that stores the story of what happened: the narrative, the content. This is not necessarily connected to the feelings. For example, "I was tortured at this time, I was this old, this is what happened".

There's another part of your brain that stores the emotions the sensations, the sounds, the smells. Now that part of your brain doesn't have a date and time stamp. It doesn't know it's 2014. So what happens is you intellectually know you're safe, you intellectually know it's 2014, but when you get triggered and the smoke alarm goes off, your brain has the sensory memories and it doesn't know that it's not now. It perceives threat as if it's happening now.

And what happens with trauma is this: Let's say a normal person is walking down an alleyway and they think they see a mugger, and they're in danger. The adrenalin system gets active, you're going to be nervous and be ready – and then you get closer and you see it's a little old lady with a hat. It's OK. Normal people get nervous, they see the threat is not real, they turn down and in a few minutes they're calm. For someone with trauma, the alarm doesn't get turned down so quickly. They get activated with the threat, but because they're so flooded and there's a lot of brain chemistry that changes, the ability to shut off and turn the alarm off takes a lot longer. You're going to feel really threatened and you're going to have the adrenalin going through your system for a lot longer.

In terms of trauma therapy, what you're doing is trying to maintain what we call 'dual awareness'. So, if you're having a flashback, the practice would be: "OK, I'm feeling really stressed, I know I'm feeling stressed because my body's really stressed, but I know it's 2014, and I'm stressed because I'm having a memory." You have to train yourself to bring yourself back into the present. There are different ways of doing this. The type of therapy I use most for trauma is EMDR (eye movement desensitisation and reprocessing) which acts on the brain's right and left

hemisphere. But yes, the brain can definitely heal
from post-traumatic stress disorder.

*HK: How long does it take on average, in your
experience, to recover?*

SK: That depends on the complexity of the trauma. If
you had a relatively healthy childhood and you have
an adult trauma then generally speaking it should be
quicker. But if you have someone who had trauma
during the developmental period, as a child whose
brain was still developing, then it's going to take a lot
longer. I couldn't really say how long: for some
people it could be really quick, a couple of months,
for other people it could be a couple of years. It
depends on the nature of the trauma, how long it
went on, whether it's someone you knew.

   An example would be: there's been a study with
political activists. Now political activists in some
countries know the threat they're under if they're
opposing the regime. They know, if I get caught, I'm
going to be imprisoned, I may be tortured. So if
they're caught, they're a little bit more robust when
it comes to having post-traumatic stress afterwards.
It's the same with people like emergency services
personnel, they don't have as much trauma as they're
prepared for it.

   Whereas people who are going about their lives
and not doing anything wrong, but are still arrested
or tortured, they are going to have a much harder
time because their illusion of safety is shattered.
They are working on the assumption, "If I play by the
rules, everything will be OK". That's not true. The
whole thing about trauma is it pierces your defences

because you're not prepared for it. That's when it can really affect you.

HK: Why does the brain create something scary, where you might think that someone is waiting outside your door? You know you're in Brighton, you're safe, but why does the brain create something false?

SK: I think it is because the brain is always trying to adapt and to learn. Think in terms of caveman days. If you're hunting and you come across a tiger and that tiger hurts you, you need to learn that a tiger in the future is going to be a threat. The thing about trauma is that when something happens, your brain doesn't store it properly. It's too overwhelming so it doesn't store the information completely, it's stored maladaptively.

I can give you an example from a case study I read about. A person was kept captive and he would hear footsteps coming to the door. The door would open and then he might get beaten, tortured, or humiliated or whatever it was. He was eventually released and he kept having panic attacks and he didn't understand why. What they figured out was that any time he heard footsteps he would have a panic attack. You might think that's ridiculous. But it's adaptive. If footsteps represent danger then your brain making something up is just classical conditioning. It creates things because it's trying to survive and protect you. Our brain is wired to avoid pain. Often with trauma it's going to interpret things incorrectly, but it's still an attempt.

HK: To what extent do you think the brain can change direction and stop focussing on negative things? To what extent can we change our own brains to think positive things?

SK: There's an interesting branch of trauma research called post-traumatic growth. The whole study is the recognition that people who go through trauma, once they work it through and get through to the other side, actually have some advantage in that they get to experience a part of themselves as more resilient and strong. They get a sense that they have got through something difficult. It might increase their compassion for other people. It might make them have more humility. There are a lot of areas where, having gone through trauma, people come out the other side and find they have grown - emotionally, psychologically, spiritually. Like a mother who loses a son to drunk drivers, and starts the Mothers Against Drunk Drivers group. Sometimes it mobilises you to do something positive, to take the pain and grief and trauma and do some positive work in the world. Not always – sometimes it breaks and alters you permanently, but often you can grow as well.

HK: Do you think when you are emotional it will help post-traumatic stress?

SK: No, I don't think so. 85 per cent of people who go through something traumatic don't go on to develop post-traumatic stress disorder. So the question is why? Why do some people get PTSD and some don't? I think there are two reasons. For some, it's because they had trauma in their past. There's something in their childhood that happened that would make them more vulnerable or susceptible to being traumatised. The other thing is that when the trauma was awful enough – torture, genocide – when it's bad enough, that's going to pretty much mess up most people.

So it's the intensity, the severity. Sometimes if it's a betrayal from a family member, which is more emotional, that's going to make you more emotional. Sometimes it's not the trauma itself; it's how you are treated by society and your culture when you come out. So if a woman's raped, that's bad enough, but it might not cause her trauma. But if she's then outcast as being no good, that secondary response may be what causes her to have trauma – so I think there's a lot of different reasons why something would be traumatic. It's not just if you're emotional. It's not a personality flaw if you get trauma. There are usually some very good reasons why.

HK: Are there any aspects of post-traumatic stress, which are 'good', which might protect your brain and help you to survive something bad?

SK: I wouldn't say there is anything from post-traumatic stress in the brain that is good. I think it's quite damaging. As I mentioned with post-traumatic growth, there can be positives there. I would say working through and getting to the other side does create some strength of character, depth of character, and could make you very robust. But when you are actually in the trauma itself, no. It's very debilitating; it can be extremely traumatic and taxing on the body and the brain.

There is an interesting study of children in
Palestine. What they were doing was providing
EMDR treatment for the kids. There were often
bombings, frequent incursions from Israeli forces,
and this would usually set them back. So they were in
the middle of this study, they were doing treatment
on the kids for the trauma, and then in the middle of
the study there was some kind of intervention and
there were Israeli forces there, shots fired and so on.
What the workers and parents said was that the kids
who would usually have regressed and had
nightmares and sleep problems, actually didn't – so
there was something about the treatment that made
them more resilient to the trauma in the present.
That's very trauma-focussed therapy, though. It
doesn't happen by itself.

The only other thing I would say is that there
was another very interesting study in Scotland. There
was some kind of disaster and a group of children
were trapped, perhaps in a bus or a mine – I don't
remember what. Years later they looked at the kids
and who developed trauma problems and who didn't.
The few people who were active in trying to get out,
who were trying to knock down walls or physically
trying to get themselves free, didn't have trauma.
The kids who sat passive or didn't do anything, who
were waiting to be rescued, they all had trauma. So
there's something about agency. If you are in the
middle of something traumatic and you feel you have
some power, that you can do something, then that
actually defends you against developing post-
traumatic stress disorder.

HK: Is there any evidence that someone who has religious faith copes better, or differently, with PTSD than someone who doesn't? Does faith help?

SK: That's a very interesting question. On the face of it, I'd say I don't know. My opinion would be that it could go both ways. If you look at the Holocaust, for some of the Jewish people who went through that, it made them lose faith in God and actually their faith made them worse: "If there's a God, then how could this happen?" Others, it kept them stronger. I wouldn't say that in and of itself religious faith is going to make you stronger, I think it really depends on how the individual uses it. It could go both ways.

HK: To what extent is it possible that survival of trauma on a community or national level can lead to long-term strength and attainment? If you look at history, black people suffered a lot of discrimination in the United States. Today America's President is black. Do you think there's a link between suffering, persecution and success?

SK: I think that's a great question. I guess if you look at history then yes, you would have to say that for any persecuted minority it creates a certain collective mobilisation towards something and it serves as a focus. Take the example of Israel. It initially started when it became a state in the '40s. The Israeli Defence Force was always used for defence. It was always being attacked by the Arab countries and so for the first 30, 40 years, it was always in defence. Now I'm Jewish so I have a bias, but if I look historically at what happened, they went from being

a country which was only using their forces to protect
and defend themselves, to being the aggressors and
actually occupying land and a people. When they
were persecuted, when they were the minority, I
think it made them stronger. Now that they are
established and secure you have an internal conflict.
It was an Israeli that killed Prime Minister Rabin
many years ago. That was one of their own. You have
the conflict between the religious and the secular,
you have people who don't believe in what they're
doing, they've had to build a wall in the country... I
wonder if there is something in being persecuted, in
the difficulties, that does create strength out of
necessity and then when they get power, it takes
difficulty to not abuse it.

*HK: People who make decisions about the economy
and justice - what kind of mentality do they have?
Does their responsibility give them a more creative
brain? Or do they already have the capability to make
this kind of decision?*

SK: I don't know that we'll ever determine that fully.
On the one level I'd say it has to do with your
upbringing. From a psychological point of view, if you
have parents or a society that's promoting justice,
equality, all that, then that's going to influence what
you believe and what you think. If you have an
educational system that's promoting tolerance, that's
going to be successful. If you have an educational
system and parents that encourage creativity, you
will get that. If you have parents that teach kids that
Jews are bad, or black people are bad, or any
prejudice, you're going to grow up with that. I think a

lot of what determines how we become is actually formed in childhood. We form those beliefs really early on, that's one layer.

Sometimes you can have one kind of upbringing but then you might have mentors or a leader, or might be influenced by a book or something else, and that can change you and influence you. So I think there are many things that will contribute to someone becoming creative. Sometimes it's hardship and trauma. Sometimes it's something else. Trauma can certainly mobilise someone to do something or be creative. But it can be something else: someone you meet, a chance encounter, a moment, a sunset, something spiritual that kind of talks to you and will shove you in a certain direction. I think it's a mystery really. But something can often spark an idea inside you.

HK: Is there anything more you would like to learn about the brain?

SK: Do you know what I'd love to know? What are the differences between men's brains and women's brains? Because we're always saying it's politically incorrect to talk about differences and I think we need to understand what our differences are, because there's so much conflict. They did a study of black cab drivers in London and found that parts of their brain are bigger because they had to memorise all the streets. I think our differences can help us and inform us.

And I think there is a way that spirituality and science can meet. Do you know the placebo effect, with medication? A placebo is basically where they do a trial for drugs. They want to know whether the drug works, so they give some people the drug and some people a sugar pill, but they don't know who has what. There's always 20 per cent of people who get better because they *think* they are taking the drug but they are not taking anything. It's the mind actually healing itself because it thinks of something. That's what I would like to know. How do we do that? How can we heal our mind just by thinking? There's no money in that because no drug companies will fund it, but that's exciting stuff, right? If 10 or 20 per cent of people can get better simply because they think they're getting something, that's exciting. That's the potential of the brain and I would love to see that explored.

HK: When you look to the future, do you think people will have more or less psychological problems than today?

SK: I think it's going to get worse. The world is really stressful. There's a lot of violence, danger, threat, uncertainty... There are so many levels of things that are stressful and damaging. Until we start educating people with emotional psychological skills from school, from the time they are small, then there are going to be tremendously more problems. We should begin to include in education skills for managing conflict, for dealing with your own emotions, teaching people mindfulness meditation, healthy lifestyles and so on. Until we get that right into the education from the time they're young, the problems are only going to get worse. There's hope, but not the way we're going now.

I left the NHS five years ago. With the economy and the downturn, I've been busy the whole time. There's been no dip. The NHS doesn't have much to offer. People are stressed, lost and confused. I think there's a huge need for psychology and it seems to be getting worse, not better.

HK: Again, looking at the future – do you think humanity will get worse or improve in the next 200 years?

SK: I think it's getting worse and better at the same time. There are many things that are wonderful; there are a lot of movements and positive social things. But I think there are a lot of really destructive things happening at the same time. I imagine it's going to get worse before it gets better. I'd like to believe that it's going to be OK, but we really haven't got a clue.

I like to think that if I look at what psychology's about, that at the core of us we're good. At the core of us is love, the desire for that sort of love and acceptance. Whether we can get to it or not I don't know, but generally speaking, people want the same thing. They want to have peace, they want to be heard, they want to be understood, they want to feel loved, they want to feel safe. I think the drive and the desire and the motivation is there. Whether we get there or not, I don't know. I can't say I'm convinced either way. But I think there's hope.

Faith, Family and New Beginnings

Farah Mohebati with Derek Parkinson

Farah is a member of the Bahá'í Faith, a religion that was founded in 1863 by the Persian nobleman, Bahá'u'lláh. The six and a half million Bahá'ís around the world today believe that all the major religions come from One God, and that all mankind belongs to one human family. Some of the teachings of the Bahá'í Faith include universal education and equality between men and women. There is no clergy or rituals in the Bahá'í Faith. Although most meetings take place in people's houses or centres, there are temples around the world open to all and their spiritual centre is in Israel. Adherents believe that Bahá'u'lláh was just the latest in a line of prophets that has included Moses, Krishna, Buddha, Zoroaster, Muhammad and Jesus.

Bahá'ís have been subject to religious persecution in various countries since the time of Bahá'u'lláh.

I'm proud of my religion because it teaches us the about the oneness of God, the oneness of religion and the unity of humanity. I've learned from my religion that I should help everybody to improve the community and humanity. In my opinion religion is good for young people. My children were brought up as Bahá'is, they are good people who have helped others a lot and supported the community.

The beginning of any new religion is often met with opposition because of resistance to change and a lack of understanding. Members of the Bahá'i Faith, including my family, have also been affected by this opposition.

My father was a third-generation Bahá'i. My paternal great-grandmother, Fatimih and her sister Bibi Sakhineh, became Bahá'is in the late 1800s. Fatimih and her husband had three children: two sons and one daughter. Her eldest son was my paternal grandfather, Ahmad Bolandipour.

Six months after Fatimih's husband passed away, a few men came to her house to warn her that people who were against the Bahá'i Faith were planning to take away her possessions and harm her and her children. They asked her for a large sum of money in return for this warning, which she gave them.

The very next evening, while all were asleep, the men she was warned about broke down the door.

Hearing the noise, my great-grandmother woke up and quickly took her children to the roof, where they watched all their possessions being taken away. One of the neighbours kindly offered her and her children a place to stay for the night. Life became very hard after that. A number of the members of the Bahá'i faith, including women and children were being harassed, tortured and killed. The cruel people who made it their mission to persecute the Bahá'is even poured boiling water down the throats of innocent babies, just because of their religion. Through her father's help, Fatimih was able to return to a certain level of normality in her life.

I was born in Persia (Iran) in a town called Yazd, on 18th July 1942. My family was very well respected and well-off. My father Fazrollah Khavari was a businessman and third-generation Bahá'i and my mother Safa Rashtizadeh was a renowned seamstress from a respected Muslim family. When they got married they had both a Baha'i and Muslim ceremony. When I was seven months old my parents went to India and for the first seven years of my life we lived in Bombay (Mumbai).

At an early age my mother had taught me many Bahá'i prayers by heart, which I would recite at different Bahá'i meetings. I remember at one such meeting where a large crowd was gathered, I was reciting a prayer standing on a table because I was so small. In the middle of the prayer I burst out in tears and could not continue. My mother, who was standing behind me, proceeded to finish the prayer for me. Those who were present were quite impressed, because she recited it so well and with such devotion even though she had only just become a Bahá'i herself.

For some time, we had a very happy and comfortable life in a lovely home by the harbour. I have many good memories of my childhood in India. I started going to preschool there, and I remember having wonderful teachers. I learned English in preschool, spoke Farsi at home and Urdu with my friends.

Then one day a few months after India's independence, when my father had just come home from work, we heard a loud explosion. We were very frightened and feared for our lives, but we ran to the roof to see what was going on. There was much confusion, but apparently a bomb had gone off on a ship that had been used in the Second World War and killed a number of people.

A few days later, on 30th January 1948, Ghandi was assassinated. After this, a lot of violence broke out between Hindus and Muslims and many people were killed. When my father was in his shop one day, he saw two men approach another outside and cut his stomach in half. The man fell to the floor and died. A war had broken out between followers of these religions, and the country was in a terrible state. It was a dangerous place for everybody, and especially for foreigners.

My father wanted to return to Iran, but as my mother was seven months pregnant and the journey by ship would be difficult for her, he decided to consult a doctor about the advisability of this move. They finally decided to leave, because even though it was a dangerous journey for her to make, it was also dangerous to remain in India. My father sold his business to a friend and we prepared to leave. All our Indian friends came to say goodbye, bringing gifts. One friend brought two garlands of flowers, placed them around my parents' necks and gave them a kiss goodbye, as was the custom in India. I was very surprised by this beautiful ceremony.

We returned to Iran when I was seven years old. I remember being very excited about traveling by ship. Many of our Persian friends were also on the same ship, although my sister and I were the only children on board. We enjoyed this initial part of the journey a lot, and would sit together in a big group listening to everyone's life stories.

We made our way to Tehran, where my maternal grandfather owned a house. The house had a lovely big garden, as well as a small swimming pool and a fountain. My aunt lived on one side of the house and we moved into the other with my grandfather.

We were very happy to be there, especially because my cousins also lived there and they were of a similar age to my sister and I. Within a few days we started attending the same school as they did. It was very close by, only a fifteen minute walk from the house. That was good, because if we were late for school we would be punished. The teacher would hit our hand with a strap and we would have to stand in the corner of the classroom.

I did not know how to write using the Farsi alphabet because I had never been to school in Iran before. My maternal uncle, Mohammed, who was in the army at the time, would hold my hand and help me write the letters. I will always remember his kindness.

I was 13 when I finished primary school, and there was a big party for all the graduating students and their parents. I was then enrolled in a well-known private school in Tehran and enjoyed my new school very much. All the students were scared of the headmistress, because she was renowned for being very strict. She was always good to me, though, because I was very well behaved.

We had 17 subjects altogether and my favourite topics were art, history and home economics. I even won a few awards for calligraphy and art. Because we lived so far from the school, I wouldn't go home over the two-hour lunch period, as other students did. I would bring my lunch with me, and, after I had eaten, I would play volleyball, basketball or table tennis with my friends. I was good at volleyball and often played with my wonderful older friend Sudabeh Hassani.

We once saw somebody take a picture of us playing volleyball but we could never find the photo. I asked at the school but nobody knew. I had no idea where that photo could have gone, but I found that same picture, by chance, some fifty years later and across the world...

* * *

My father owned a timber merchant business in Tehran which over the years became very successful, later expanding to include a joinery. My family usually spent the summers in the north of Persia on the shores of the Caspian Sea. Beside the beautiful natural vegetation there, the area was covered with large fields of a lovely rich green colour. There were tea plantations, rice fields and thousands of citrus fruit trees - oranges, lemons and tangerines. Because it was a woman's job to gather the crops, they could often be seen in the fields wearing beautiful, colourful dresses. We also visited the large tea factories nearby and were fascinated by observing how tea was made. The seaside itself was breathtaking in its beauty, with miles of undisturbed sand, crystal clear waters and blue skies. I really loved it there.

When I turned sixteen, I came home from school one day to find we had some special visitors. My mother told me they were relatives of ours and had brought us a beautiful basket of flowers, as was the custom in Persia. She told me the gentleman, whose name was Habib, had noticed me at a wedding, and would very much like to ask for my hand in marriage. I was a bit surprised, because I felt I was too young to get married.

Habib and his sister came back to visit us a number of times, always bringing a gift of flowers. On one of those occasions we had the chance to talk, and I agreed to marry him. In order for a Bahá'í marriage to take place, the parents of both the bride and groom need to give their consent for the marriage. During the ceremony itself the bride and groom repeat the prescribed marriage verse, "We will all, verily, abide by the will of God", in the presence of two witnesses.

Our wedding took place three months after our engagement. The beautiful Bahá'í ceremony took place at my parents' home. A marriage prayer was read, and Habib and I repeated the marriage verse. In the afternoon we had a big reception in my aunt's garden with 400 friends and relatives. Colourful lights were placed on each tree and a very long table was set up to serve dinner to all the guests. Two famous singers performed for us and we enjoyed the wonderful music. After dinner we cut our four-tiered wedding cake decorated with flowers. Interestingly, some American film-makers who were making a movie about Iranian culture and were being hosted by my Aunt, asked if they could also film my wedding. We agreed and they gave my Aunt a copy of the film. We went on honeymoon to Shiraz, another large city in Iran. We were soon blessed with our daughter, Farahnaz. Nine years later our son Fariborz was born and three years later we welcomed our youngest son, Farzad.

I have a memory of visiting one of my relatives in Yazd one summer. I saw a lady begging outside, the weather was hot and she had no water or anything. I took some watermelon out to her and talked with her. She was magnificent; she said that even ash in my hand would turn into a jewel. She was so kind and nice. I was just 17 years old then. I felt that my life changed after this meeting; whatever step I took it was a step for the good. I don't know why, but I think it must have been from the spirit of this lady, that things have been good for me ever since.

* * *

Whilst in Tehran I used to be a teacher and also did a lot for the community, helping elderly people and people who needed support. My husband also supported a lot of relatives and family.

When my daughter was 17, she married a young doctor and a few years later had two children. My two sons went to school at the Andisheh School in Tehran. It was established by Italian people and was a private school. A few years later, my parents, who were then retired, moved to England around 1976.

In 1979, the Iranian Revolution happened. My sons' school was closed down as the authorities thought it was conspiring against Iran because it was lavish and had money. The school was beautiful and they had Farsi language half the day and English the other half. Everybody was happy there but we didn't have any choice when they closed it.

I had planned to come to England on holiday for many years, and we already had a house in Hollingbury to stay in when we arrived. One of our relatives had seen the house for sale and encouraged us to buy it many years earlier. The British embassy in Iran was shut down after the revolution and we couldn't get a visa so we decided to go to Germany and get a visa from there to travel to England. In those days we were free to go to Germany without a visa.

The night after we left on holiday, Tehran airport was destroyed by Iraq. This was the start of the Iraq/Iran war. Soon after that the Iranian government confiscated my husband's hardware store and our home because of our Faith.

We arrived in Germany and my husband's cousin and his German wife Maria were waiting for us at Munich airport. We couldn't speak German so we had to rely on my husband's cousin to translate for us when we spoke with others. We were fortunate to have been able to rent the same house we had stayed in when we visited Germany many years before. The house had a beautiful balcony and we had a lovely time eating there together.

We stayed there for three months because it took that long to get our British visas, as our names were written using the Farsi alphabet in our Iranian passports and needed to be officially translated. We had to go to Frankfurt embassy several times to check how the process was going.

It was winter by the time we got our visa and had started to snow but it was beautiful to be in Germany for Christmas.

All the time we were thinking about my daughter. She was still in Iran with her two children and we were very worried about her.

Finally we reached our house in Brighton. Although my parents were living in Brighton as well, they decided they wanted to move to Canada. They were able to get a visa and soon found a flat in Hamilton, near Toronto. Unfortunately we could not visit them at all because we were not able to get a visa.

My daughter, son-in-law and two sisters left Iran as well and went to Pakistan.

My father was very upset because he wanted to support his family but it was too much and after eight months he had a heart attack and passed away. My mother was left alone: she could not come to England. Fortunately some Canadian Bahá'is were able to help her, and one of my sisters who used to work in the American embassy in Tehran and had studied in England and America was able to get a visa and come to her assistance.

* * *

When we came to England I started to go to college to improve my English. I attended twice a week. My husband and I went together but he had never studied English before, and so I was quite a lot further ahead than him. As my English was good, I decided to volunteer at one of the local schools, then called the Davigdor School. I was an assistant teacher from 9am to 4pm, twice a week. Once the headmistress Mrs Penny tried to give me an envelope full of money, but I refused to open it. I couldn't work in England at that time because I didn't have a permanent passport, but I didn't mind giving my time voluntarily. I urged her to give the money to the school. She was extremely surprised, and said I was a unique lady.

I also took a 12-week business course. Everyone else was British, but it was an amazing experience and I will never forget it. At the end I brought flowers and dishes of Persian food and everyone was appreciative. The group of twelve of us remained friends after this and continued to meet. I have also kept in touch with the Mayor, who presented us with certificates.

There were also a lot of activities at the local Bahá'í Centre in Stanford Avenue in Brighton. An English Bahá'í friend, Jenny, welcomed our children to the Bahá'í Sunday School there. The centre was

built in Victorian times. The Bahá'i couple who owned
it donated it to the community when they moved to
Australia. It's a really beautiful house. The windows
of the house are stained glass and the ceiling is
beautiful and intricate. There are a lot of activities
there and every nineteen days the whole community
meets together to pray, to consult and to socialize.
The children also share what they had been doing in
their Sunday School classes, including arts and
singing. The centre also helped to establish interfaith
meetings with different faiths all coming together. I
was one of the early members of the Interfaith group
in Brighton.

During this time we also invited some of our
neighbours to come for tea or Persian food and we
had a lovely time together. I remember one of our
new neighbours who were very kind. We became very
close to them, and would visit each other and have
our children play together. There was a street party
on our road and it was amazing to have all the
neighbours together. It took place in all of the
gardens and alleyways behind the houses. The
atmosphere was very friendly and we all enjoyed
spending time together and getting closer.

My parents had organised a school for my two
sons near our place before we came to England. They
had been lucky, but after a while we got a letter from
the Home Office saying we should send our sons to
private school instead of the public school. We went
to talk to the headmaster to try and ask if we could
pay but it was not possible, and they had to go to a
private school. Unfortunately we couldn't find
anywhere in Brighton so they ended up going to
Shoreham College. My husband had to take them to

school every day and it was a long journey to do
before 9 o'clock in the morning.

When my sons started at Shoreham College, my
eldest did not have any problems studying in English,
because he had learned the language in Iran.
However, my youngest had never studied English
before and had to work very hard until he improved.
During the weekend they were taught Farsi too – we
had a private teacher to come and help them. My
oldest son became fluent in Farsi and he took and
passed an exam in London. But my youngest son did
not have the time to carry on with both languages
because he had a lot of other studying to do. Both of
them loved football and cricket, though. They would
play non-stop during their time off.

Ever since I came to England I have tried to help
people where I can. I was one of a number of people
who received a special cup from the Mayor at a
presentation at the Pavilion in recognition of
volunteering in the community. The Pavilion is my
favourite place in Brighton because the Mayor once
invited the Interfaith Committee to a dinner there. A
representative of the Queen was present and it was
the first time all the faiths were together in the
Pavilion. It was really magnificent.

But it was Brighton Library that gave me one of
my biggest surprises. Although the photo of my
friend Sudabeh and me playing volleyball had been
lost for many years I had not forgotten it.
International Women's day was coming up and the
chair lady asked me to make a story of my country. I
went to the library to do some research and I spotted

the picture! Can you believe it? After all those years, and in Brighton Library!

Farah playing volleyball in Iran

The Trial: Franz Kafka and the UK Asylum Process

Stephen Silverwood

It has become a journalistic cliché to refer to the life of an asylum seeker as 'Kafkaesque'. But what do we mean when we say this? And what does it tell us about the asylum process? Is it just the twists and turns and dead ends of the bureaucracy? Or are there similarities too in the brutal 'justice' of The Penal Colony, the absurdity of The Bridge, the transformation of the Metamorphosis and in the destitution of The Hunger Artist?

The World of Franz Kafka
"A book must be the axe for the frozen sea within us" (Kafka, 1904).

Franz Kafka was a writer who lived in Prague in the early 20th Century. He was part of the Jewish minority in the city and suffered feelings of alienation and depression throughout his life. He never married and died at the age of 40 from starvation, brought about by tuberculosis. He was unknown in his own lifetime.

After Kafka's death, his short stories started to become popular. They were characterised by confused heroes drifting through absurd situations, like Gregor Samsa in *Metamorphosis*, who awakens one morning to discover he has turned into a giant insect. In Kafka's novel, *The Castle*, he tells the story of a land surveyor who is summoned to a village by the mysterious authorities of a nearby castle. The protagonist spends the entire novel trying and failing to reach them. He never gets to the castle.

Kafka's outlook on life greatly influenced existentialist thinkers such as Jean Paul Sartre and Albert Camus. In his essay, *The Myth of Sisyphus,* Camus philosophises on the mythical Greek hero who was condemned to push a boulder up a mountain only to see it roll down again, over and over for eternity. This metaphor for the absurdity of human existence is the same as Kafka's Castle, but in Kafka's work the forces of frustration are not gravity and the gods but the oblique power of bureaucracy.

Kafka's most famous work is *The Trial* (originally published in German as *Der Process*). This tells the story of Josef K., a bank clerk who is arrested and prosecuted by a remote, inaccessible authority for a crime that is never revealed. Throughout the novel, Josef K. attempts to navigate a labyrinthine system of secret courts and unknown rules. Just like the hero of *The Castle*, Josef K. fails. No actual trial ever takes place and the novel ends with his execution. As he is stabbed through the heart, Josef's last words are *"Like a dog!"*.

These nightmarish tales of individual helplessness in the face of a complex bureaucracy gave birth to the term 'Kafkaesque'. This has been used to describe similar narratives, such as *The Prisoner,* a 1960s television serial about a former spy trapped in a bizarre village, and *Brazil,* the 1985 Terry Gilliam film about a doomed bureaucrat in a future British dystopia. The term can also be used to describe 'catch-22' situations, where an individual is faced with a choice of actions, but has no hope of winning.

The Trial

"The flood of the Revolution evaporates, and leaves behind only the slime of a new bureaucracy. The chains of tormented mankind are made out of red tape" (Kafka, 1927).

To anyone who has been through the asylum process, this will sound all-too familiar. Far from the image presented in the tabloid media of asylum seekers exploiting the system for their own gain, the reality for most people is one of being a *victim* of the system. This is the story told to us at Refugee Radio over and over again by the people we have interviewed over the years. The Home Office and its immigration department, the UK Visas and Immigration[1], are the archetypal faceless institutions. Most of the human contact with the Home Office takes the form of uniformed enforcement officers and security guards,

---

1 Immigration enforcement is the subject of frequent reorganisations by the government. Prior to March 2013, the work was done by an executive agency, the UK Border Agency (UKBA). After a damning report on the agency it was announced that it would be split, with UK Visas and Immigration focusing on the visa system and border enforcement being done by the UK Border Force.

most of whom work for private security companies
such as the infamous global corporation G4S, and so
are not even actual employees of the state. By far
most of the contact is in writing. That is, writing *from*
the Home Office, though, not writing *to* them. Almost
every letter sent to the Home Office goes
unanswered. If they are confronted with the
situation, they will deny ever receiving the letter, to
the extent that all correspondence ends up being sent
by recorded delivery - and even this is not failsafe.

Information given out is fragmented and
contradictory. Internal phone numbers are kept
secret and regularly changed. Letters are generally
unsigned and few if any officers involved with a case
will reveal their names. Documents are frequently
lost and files misplaced, sometimes for years. All
attempts at communication are futile. The only thing
to do is sit in limbo and wait: for a knock on the door
in the middle of the night from a removal squad, or
the heavy thud of another fatal Home Office envelope
through the letterbox.

Most of the letters sent from the Home Office
are arbitrary instructions for 'reporting'. This is a
process whereby asylum seekers are forced to visit
an unwelcoming Reporting Centre and sign
documents to demonstrate they have not absconded.
People are variously instructed to sign monthly,
weekly or even daily in some cases. This can involve
expensive and time-consuming journeys to and from
the centres - those living in Brighton, for example,
must travel to London to report. People are forced to
queue up in overcrowded corrals before being taken
off for fingerprinting or other biometric probes. The
centres are sinister places. Asylum seekers have told

us that, every time they report, there is the possibility they will be taken away without warning and imprisoned in a detention centre. Some charitable organisations, such as the Unity Centre in Glasgow, have been forced to set up buddy systems for reporting because of this possibility.

Kafka's Josef K. was prosecuted for a crime that was never revealed and had quite possibly never occurred. Similarly in the asylum system, individuals and families who have committed no crime can be detained at any time, in what are effectively prisons, for 'administrative convenience'. In these detention centres they are kept locked up and prevented from leaving. They are barred from accessing most of the internet, including immigration websites, advice charities, Facebook and other social networking sites. They are barred from talking to the press or having their photograph taken. They do not know when they will be released. The detention is 'indefinite' and in many cases can last for years.

These are the fortunate ones. The unlucky ones will be 'removed', or deported. This is done by the same private security companies who run the detention centres for profit: controversial multinational corporations such as GSL, GEO and G4S. The prisons seem to change hands between the companies as often as the companies change their names. According to Dr Frank Arnold of the charity, Medical Justice, the bids to undertake the work are afforded to the cheapest provider. The government aims to pay as little as possible; the companies want to make profits. There is a conflict between the duty to provide adequate services and the commercial drive on both sides: in this case, profits come far

before people. The set-up offers a convenient excuse
for the government to say, "It's not our fault: it's the
detention centre," and the detention centre to say,
"It's not our fault: it's the government". It becomes
what Dr Arnold has called a circular firing squad. In
2010, the company G4S alone received 775
complaints including physical and sexual assault and
racism. In 2011, the Prisons Inspector described
conditions in a G4S immigration centre as
"objectionable, distressing [and] inhumane".

In 2010, the Institute of Race Relations
produced a damning report on the deaths of asylum
seekers, and the government policies which put
vulnerable people at risk. It reported that 77 asylum
seekers and migrants had died in the preceding five
years, of whom 44 died as an indirect consequence of
the iniquities of the asylum system. Other groups put
the figure much higher. For example, the website for
campaign group No Deportations lists 1,367
attempted suicides alone in detention centres during
the past five years.

In 2012, a 31-year-old Ghanaian man called
Prince Ofosu died after being 'restrained' by GEO
Group staff at Harmondsworth Immigration Removal
Centre (IRC). A statement from other Ghanaian
detainees at the centre alleges that Ofosu sustained
massive blows from one officer who later asked to
change his "blood stained clothes so that no one
would notice what happened", and that the officer
concerned is now on leave "in order to pervert the
course of justice". After the beating, which happened
in a solitary confinement room, they say that they
were told by another officer who was present that
Ofosu was stripped naked, the heating was turned

off, and he was "left in the cold without even a duvet till his death 24 hours after being detained at the block". The statement also makes allegations about the mistreatment of other Ghanaians, and the lack of proper medical care at the centre where there is no permanent doctor (as is frequently the case at detention centres). There appears to have been no proper police investigation of his death, which has been referred to the Prisons and Probation Ombudsman.

The asylum seekers we have spoken to tell us that they are also invariably mistreated during removal. They are racially abused and beaten by the guards, sometimes in the van on the way to the aeroplane, sometimes on the plane itself and sometimes in the van on the way back to the centre from the plane - occasionally flights are postponed if the pilot objects too much to all the violence. A Cameroonian man who was trafficked into slavery as a child told us he was punched in the groin and needed medical attention. Another Cameroonian man, Marius Betondi, was beaten so hard he received serious injuries to his eyes and face. Seven months later, an Angolan man, Jimmy Mubenga, was killed by three G4S guards at the same airport. *"Like a dog!"*

A Hunger Artist
"So long as you have food in your mouth, you have solved all questions for the time being." (Kafka, 1922).

Bureaucratic processes and cruelty are not the only links with the work of Franz Kafka. Considered together, his writings outline a reality of existential suffering and pain that describe other aspects of the asylum experience.

Kafka died in a Viennese sanatorium in 1924. He was suffering from laryngeal tuberculosis which made his throat so painful that he could not eat. He eventually died of starvation. At the time of his death, Kafka was revising a short story entitled *A Hunger Artist*, or *Ein Hungerkünstler*. The story was about a circus performer who would entertain crowds by prolonged bouts of fasting in a cage. When the public bores of him, the hunger artist is sidelined and forgotten. He embarks on an endless fast and his emaciated corpse is finally discovered by an overseer who is cleaning out the dirty straw from his apparently empty cage. The hunger artist is buried and replaced by a panther.

Hunger and destitution is always a threat for asylum seekers, a far cry from the headlines in the tabloid press about asylum seekers on benefits living the 'high life' at the tax payers expense. (A typical *Daily Mail* headline from January 2014 read 'The "destitute" asylum seekers with luxury TVs and iPads'.) This is the antithesis to the experience of hundreds of people pushed into the shadows by the asylum system. They are left homeless and hungry, sometimes compelled to beg or forced into prostitution. The more that the public hear about "bogus asylum seekers" and "welfare cheats" in the press, the more pressure the politicians put on the system to be 'tough' and the more innocent people suffer.

Asylum seekers are not entitled to work or claim welfare benefits. They have to wait months or years for a decision to be made on their claim and in the meantime they have to live on handouts. One Zimbabwean woman who accessed a local church group in Brighton complained to Refugee Radio about living in "limbo" and told us "You just have to sit and rot... like a cabbage". If their claim for asylum is refused, or perhaps just because of some administrative error, all of their support will be stopped. This does not mean that they were lying about their reasons for claiming asylum: over a quarter of all cases refused by the Home Office are overturned on appeal on the basis that the initial decision was incorrect. Even those who never get a positive answer often have legitimate claims – the system is skewed against people, designed to be unfair for political motives of reducing numbers given refugee status. This does not mean that they can just 'go home'. Sometimes they cannot be removed even if they wanted to because we do not have an embassy in their country, it is impossible for the Home Office to secure the necessary travel documents, or because it is too dangerous to fly there due to a war. Sometimes they are deported into a similar situation in another EU country, such as Italy or Greece, because that is where they have previously been fingerprinted. Many are left on the streets to starve in the hope that they will just disappear.

They are also prevented from accessing healthcare. We spoke to one man in Brighton who was turfed out of a hospital bed and had his oxygen mask removed when it was discovered he was a foreign national. He was then sent a bill for thousands of pounds which he tried to pay through loans, even though he had no income and was not allowed to work. We know of other people who have come to the end of their asylum claims but have life-threatening illnesses, the treatment for which is not available in their home country. When that treatment is removed in the UK, it is with the effect of using the NHS as a stick.

All of the institutions in the UK that a British citizen experiences as benign can be used to make life untenable for asylum seekers in order to drive them out of the country. This includes things like social services, who now have the power to remove people's children from them if they do not immediately comply with directions to leave the country. So, if you are not starved or diseased into defeat, then there are other processes available to the people who control the institutions from their remote offices, just like the men in Kafka's inaccessible Castle.

Metamorphosis

"As Gregor Samsa awoke one morning from uneasy dreams he found himself transformed in his bed into a gigantic insect" (Kafka, 1915).

Like Gregor Samsa, the asylum seeker experiences a change of states during the process from human to being treated as something less than human. This is ironic as so many asylum seekers have fled to the UK in search of sanctuary after having been denied their human rights in their country of origin.

Even if an asylum seeker's claim is successful and they become a refugee, and even if they later go on to become a British citizen, there still remains some indefinable aura of this process of humiliation and dehumanisation in their relationship with their new home. It is as if the toll of spending years in the soul-grinding oppression of stateless limbo produces a corrosive effect on individual powers of resilience that is singular and distinct from the experience of someone who has merely migrated from one country to another.

In the Penal Colony

"One is no longer ashamed of wanting to die; one asks to be moved from the old cell, which one hates, to a new one, which one will only in time come to hate" (Kafka, 1918).

This difference is even apparent between two people who have both experienced torture or some other trauma, where one has been through the asylum process and the other has not. In this sense the asylum process is a kind of secondary, or additional trauma. Again, this is often ironic as it is a bureaucratic violence inflicted by the British state on people who have fled torture and persecution by their own states, and sought refuge in the home of what centuries of colonial propaganda has taught them is 'Great British Justice'.

Kafka writes about torture in his short story, *In the Penal Colony*. In this story another bemused hero drifts through another absurd nightmare of authoritarian horror. A traveller arrives on a prison island where a man known as 'the Officer' demonstrates an elaborate torture device, the Harrow, which carves the sentence of a condemned prisoner onto their skin as they die painfully over several hours. The traveller is appalled but the

Officer insists that the condemned undergo a moment of enlightenment on the nature of justice in their final moments. When the traveller refuses to advocate the use of the Harrow, the Officer hurls himself into the machine to have the words "BE JUST" carved into his back so that he too can experience the transformation. The Harrow, however, malfunctions and the Officer is instantly killed.

The harrowing of asylum seekers by the immigration system can be equally deadly. They arrive in the UK with a history of trauma behind them and a battle ahead of them. Refugees are nearly twice as likely to experience mental health problems than the national average.[2] Post-traumatic stress disorder (PTSD) is especially prevalent as a result of torture, sexual violence and war in their home countries.[3] . Recent research by the Department of Social Policy and Intervention at the University of Oxford indicates that one third of asylum seeking children are likely to suffer from PTSD.[4]

For those who have survived persecution and who can navigate the asylum process to make a new

---

2   Tribe, R. (2002) 'Mental Health of Refugees and Asylum-Seekers', *Journal of Advances In Psychiatric Treatment,* Vol 8: p.240-247; Department Of Health (2011), '*No Health Without Mental Health: A Cross-Government Mental Health Outcomes Strategy For People Of All Ages*'.
3   Migrant & Refugee Communities Forum & CVS Consultants, (2002)' *A Shattered World: The Mental Health Needs Of Refugees And Newly Arrived Communities*
4   Bronstein, I., Montgomery, P. & Dobrowolski, S. (2012). PTSD in Asylum-Seeking Male Adolescents from Afghanistan. *Journal of Traumatic Stress.* Volume 25. (Issue 5).p. 551-557.

home in the UK, their past experiences can even help them to develop resilience and withstand future pressures. For those who are left living in limbo with an uncertain fate or those who are imprisoned for years, however, it seems that past traumas only contribute to higher vulnerability, sometimes resulting in self-harm and suicide.

The list of victims is long. For example: Bereket Yohannes from Eritrea, 26, was found hanged in the showers at Harmondsworth IRC. Manuel Bravo from Angola was found hanging in the stairwell at Yarl's Wood IRC. Ramazan Kumluca, 19, a Kurdish asylum seeker from Turkey, was found hanged in Campsfield House IRC. Kenny Peter from Nigeria, jumped to his death in Colnbrook IRC after being hospitalised for self-harm. Tran Quang Tung from Vietnam, 23, was found hanged in Dungavel IRC. Sergey Barnuyck, 31, a Ukrainian, was found hanged in Harmondsworth. Mikhail Bognarchuk, 42, a Ukrainian asylum seeker, was found hanged at Haslar IRC. Robertas Grabys, a Lithuanian asylum seeker, was found hanged in Harmondsworth on the day he was due to be deported. Kimpua Nsimba, 24, a Congolese asylum seeker was also found hanged in Harmondsworth. It transpired that no-one had even spoken to him in over four days.

By contrast, Kafka's Penal Colony seems positively enlightened. The Harrow has fallen into disuse and the influential traveller does not want to see it brought back. Public disgust has brought about an end to the practice. Another difference lies in the Officer's insistence that the cruelty of the machine is in some way beneficial to the prisoner. He is not just a sadist. He believes the Harrow offers some kind of

salvation whereas the Home Secretary's stated aim is
to make Britain a "hostile environment" for
undesirable migrants. The discourse of tabloid
newspapers and the politicians is to call for "tougher"
measures against the "tides" of asylum seekers.
Stories of individual suffering and suicide rarely elicit
concern or calls for change to the process. These
tragic victims are the casualties of "toughness". The
UK has become a prison island, run by private
companies, driven by isolationist opinion-makers,
exacting a shadowy psychological discipline against
people with no voice. "BE JUST", indeed.

The Bridge
*"Plenty of hope, an infinite amount of hope—but not
for us"* (Kafka, 1937).

Kafka's most famous novel is *The Trial*. The title in
German is *Der Process*, and in fact the English word
'process' may be even more telling than the more
commonly translated term 'trial'. At the heart of
Kafka's work is the totalising bureaucratic *process*:
not just the system itself but the *way* the system
operates.

One example of how this relates to the public's
attitude to asylum is Kafka's less well-known short
story, *The Bridge*. In *The Bridge*, Kafka writes from
the first person perspective of a bridge stretched
across a ravine. A mysterious person walks across the
bridge and starts to jump. The bridge is worried that
it could be a suicide and turns around to see who it
is, breaking itself up and falling apart in the process,
to be smashed onto the rocks below.

Kafka died before the rise of the Nazis in Germany and did not witness the impact of the Holocaust on the Jewish community in Prague and upon his own family. Kafka's sisters, Elli and Valli, were sent with their children to the Łódź Ghetto in Poland. Known to the Germans as the Litzmannstadt Ghetto, it was the second largest after Warsaw. Originally part of the city of Łódź, the Germans encircled the Ghetto with wire fences and sealed the Jews inside. During the war around 200,000 Jews and Roma passed through the Ghetto. Most, including Elli and Valli, did not survive.

Kafka's beloved youngest sister, Ottla, was sent to the concentration camp at Theresienstadt. On 7th October 1943, Ottla accompanied a group of children as a voluntary assistant to Auschwitz. There she was murdered by the Nazis in the gas chambers, along with over a million others.

One of the most disturbing points of the camps is not just that they happened, but that the mass of ordinary Germans knew they were happening at the time and did nothing to prevent them.

A Canadian professor called Robert Gellately wrote a book revealing that, far from a state secret, the German newspapers in fact regularly reported on news of the camps.[5] It was widely accepted that the camps were needed to permanently detain the "subhumans".[6] Everything but the gas chambers themselves was common public knowledge, and it is still unclear how many people knew about the full extent of the Final Solution. Public support for the death penalty was certainly high, with large numbers

5   Gellately, R (2001) *Backing Hitler*, Oxford University Press.
6   Ibid.

of people attending the public executions of foreign workers found guilty of criminal acts. There was no united resistance movement against the Nazis in Germany.

This national failure to challenge the system presents a moral challenge to history. Once a group of people are demonised and rendered subhuman then the public becomes incapable of seeing their plight. It becomes as absurd and unlikely as the idea of a bridge turning around to see the person walking across its back.

This process is happening right now on an industrial scale in Burma. There are similar processes in Syria, Sudan (Darfur) and the Democratic Republic of Congo. Other recent instances of genocide include the Serbian rape camps in Kosovo and the death of a million people in Rwanda. All of these resulted in people being forcibly displaced within their own countries. Some of them spilled into neighbouring countries to live in semi-permanent refugee camps. An even smaller percentage fled to Europe to seek asylum, and an even smaller percentage fled to the UK. Of these, a large number were detained.

In the most recent year there were 20,000 claims for asylum. In the same year there were 30,000 people in immigration detention. These numbers speak for themselves.

When one wonders how the people of Burma can continue to turn a blind eye to the genocide within their own country, or how it felt to live in Nazi Germany and not care about the reality of the concentration camps, it makes one think about the people living in the UK today and the way we all view the asylum system.

Of course there is a difference between a concentration camp and a detention centre, but the *process* is unchanged.

From Cameroon's prisons to UK detention: Where are the human rights?

Robert Miki Tamanji, Ivo Kuka & Lorna Stephenson

The stories of Refugee Radio contributors Robert Miki Tamanji and Ivo Kuka, from Cameroon, follow a similar trajectory. As with hundreds of other activists like them, who campaign for independence for the anglophone region of Southern Cameroon, their political activities have put them in extreme danger. The regime brutally represses the movement, subjecting non-violent activists to harassment, torture and imprisonment.

When remaining in Cameroon became untenable, both fled to Europe and sought asylum in the UK as political refugees. Reeling from their ordeals in Cameroon, neither was prepared for the suffering they would go on to experience in the UK asylum system. As seasoned campaigners, both were keen to speak out about the injustice they've seen inside and outside of Cameroon. Later in this chapter, Robert shares his political background and explains what led him to seek sanctuary in the UK, while Ivo describes his experience of the 'fast-track' process in detention.

President Paul Biya's regime, the anglophone movement and human rights

"We have no rights, we have no dignity as human beings back in our country. That's why we are here today and until we have our freedom we will never give up. Just like the South Africans did for 27 years and now they are free. Southern Cameroonians have been enslaved for 50 years. We know in our souls, in our hearts and in our minds: We will be free. It's all we need. Freedom is what we need. The whole world must come to the plight of Southern Cameroonians. We must be free. We must be free. We must be free."

Last October, along with the 1st Octobers for many years before, Southern Cameroonians living in the UK protested outside Downing Street. The small group gathered, chanting for independence, holding placards and listening to speeches about their little-known cause, before presenting a petition to the British government. The protest also called for the British to protect Cameroonian asylum seekers who are members of the Southern Cameroons National Council (SCNC). So far they have received no such assurance.

The indifference to the cause that the British government has shown so far belies its role in the roots of the problem. The area, formerly British Southern Cameroon under colonial rule, gained

independence on 1st October 1961. But the UK, as an
administering body, failed to ensure Southern
Cameroonians got a lasting, complete resolution or to
prevent the process being hijacked. It was divided,
with the western part joining Nigeria, and the
eastern part joining La Republique Du Cameroun,
which had become independent from France the year
before.

The autonomous status enjoyed at first by
Southern Cameroon within La Republique was short-
lived. The government increased its grip of power
and soon replaced the federal constitution with a
unitary one, a process Southern Cameroonians view
as annexation. The process was completed when
President Paul Biya came to power in 1982 and
formed a one-party and centralised state. Despite
officially moving towards a multi-party system in the
years since, Biya's hold on power has remained
undisputed and he retains the power to control
legislation and rule by decree. As demonstrators at
Downing Street explained, Southern Cameroonians
are not represented in parliament, their rights are
not respected and the region has been "colonised" by
military troops. As one attendee put it, "We have
used all peaceful means. We don't want a massacre in
Cameroon, that's the way it is going. We don't want
Rwanda in Cameroon".

The repression of Southern Cameroonian
activists has only increased in recent years. The
SCNC was formed in 1995 and the efforts of
Southern Cameroonians focussed on independence
and not just autonomy. The Council, an umbrella
organisation for student and trade unions and
political groups, was targeted by security forces.

Activists were subjected to individual and mass arrests, and political activities were routinely disrupted. In the 2000s the SCNC - a non-violent movement - was declared illegal.

The context of the movement is far from liberal or democratic. For a country largely left alone and viewed as 'stable' in the eyes of the West and the former colonisers in particular, the grievances against the government are multiple. The Biya government harasses and imprisons journalists, restricts freedoms of speech and association, and impedes freedom of movement. Corruption is pervasive at all levels. Societal violence and discrimination against women and girls - including female genital mutilation - is a major problem, as is the trafficking of children and discrimination against pygmies, gay men and lesbians. The government has restricted workers' rights and the activities of unions while hereditary servitude, forced labour and child labour continue.

The most important problems, however, are the human rights abuses at the hands of the security forces. According to the UN, there are continued reports that security forces tortured, beat, harassed, and otherwise abused citizens, prisoners, and detainees. This includes women, children and the elderly. In 2010, 296 police officers and 115 soldiers and gendarmes were sanctioned or prosecuted for misconduct.[1] Eight security force members were tried for torture the same year, of whom two were

---

1   United States Department of State, *2011 Human Rights report: Cameroon,* 24 May 2012:
http://www.state.gov/j/drl/rls/hrrpt/2011/af/186173.htm

convicted, two were acquitted, and four cases are pending.

These small numbers mask a much larger problem. Numerous international human rights organisations and some prison personnel report that torture is widespread. During a 2009 visit to New Bell Prison in Douala, foreign government officials found that prison guards chained disobedient and violent prisoners in a tiny disciplinary cell, where they were reportedly beaten and denied access to food. Security forces reportedly stripped prisoners and detainees, confined them in severely overcrowded cells, denied them access to toilets or other sanitation facilities, and beat them to extract confessions or information about alleged criminals.

* * *

It was in these horrific circumstances like this that both Robert and Ivo – along with many other campaigners with the SCNC over the years - found themselves.

The Story of Robert Miki Tamanji

"My problems with the Cameroon authorities started in 1991 at the University of Yaoundé, when I was the spokesman for the Student Union called 'le Parlement' (the assembly). I was also the leader of the University Human Rights club. Because of my involvement in student politics, I endured immense persecution - ranging from arbitrary arrest, to detention, torture and imprisonment. Throughout my university years, I was arrested in three different instances and detained by the Gendarmes, the police and the secret police agents.

"In February 1992 in Yaoundé, I took part in a peaceful demonstration denouncing the government's poor human right records and especially the treatment of the Anglophone students at the University of Yaoundé. Being the leader of the Human Rights club, I championed this cause. I was targeted for my opinions and was arrested, detained and tortured for four months at the Kondengui prison, a high security prison for political dissidents.

"While in detention I was subjected to inhumane treatment. I was stripped naked and tortured with police belts, kicked and punched repeatedly. I was given electric shocks and asked to sleep on a cement floor littered with very cold water. I sustained a lot of injuries as a result of the severe torture bestowed on me by the Secret Service. I was raped many times. The conditions in the cell were disgusting, despicable and awful. There was no electricity, no beds, and no toilets and I was not given any access to medical treatment despite my deplorable health condition. I was photographed and my details taken and sent to the Presidency and I was told, categorically, that I will never work in Cameroon.

"My release was only possible, along with the release of some others, by the intervention of the Cameroon Human Rights Commission and its then president, Dr Solomon Forgwe. Dr Forgwe was also then detained for some time.

"On the 28th June 1992, I was again brutally arrested and detained at the Yaoundé central police station for three months. This time it was because I participated in a public rally and demonstration in which I spoke about the Anglophone oppression and marginalisation, and their rights to self-determination, which is a fundamental human right. Behind closed doors in appalling cell conditions, others protesters and I were tortured with impunity by the police and the Secret Service, including the Gendarmes. I was frequently beaten with iron rods, military belts and asked to stand in a pool of water for long hours while naked. Having food once a day in detention was a luxury.

"In September 1992, I was again arbitrarily and brutally arrested for five months in Bonamoussadi, the student residential quarters in Yaoundé, where I was speaking to 'le Parlement'. During this demonstration we called on the Cameroon government to put an end to bribery and corruption, dictatorship and electoral fraud. I experienced severe torture for exposing and criticising the government and the president. While naked on a cold cement floor, many police officers began kicking me all over my body. At the same time others were throwing hot water into my eyes, which has resulted in me developing eye problems which I still have today. At this same demonstration many students were killed.

"I continued to endure severe brutalisation, detention and torture between 1992 and 1994. I was on many occasions in detention at different police stations for standing out and criticising the government. Sometimes I was detained for three months, four months, six months, ten months and for a year. From 1994, I became a prominent, dedicated and active member of SCNC (Southern Cameroons National Council) a non-violent Anglophone movement. The Council peacefully seeks the independence of the former UN trust territory under British rule, called British Southern Cameroon, that has been colonised, annexed and occupied by the government of La Republique. My involvement in this cause equally exposed me to the Cameroon authorities. In 1995 and 1996, I was arrested many times and detained with torture alongside other SCNC activists as we participated in many SCNC demonstrations.

"In 1997 I was arrested in my house one morning at about 4am, accused of instigating secession after a lecture I gave my students of Kemonde Secondary School in Victoria. I was interrogated for several hours by the Secret Service about the content of my lectures. I was in detention for ten months. In 1998, during our bi-monthly meeting of SCNC Victoria South District where I was the coordinator, I was arrested at about 3pm with other SCNC members and taken to the Buea police station. We were detained for six months and later charged for 'instigating secession', belonging to an illegal organisation, and causing public disorder. I was taken to court in Buea and sentenced to four years in prison with other members. The first three years I spent in Buea prison, before being transferred to New Bell prison in Douala.

"I have lots of nightmares and hallucinations to this day because of the torture and incarceration I have endured over the years in the hands of the

Cameroon government. I hope this will help throw
some light on the ordeal I have been through."

* * *

'Fast Track': The two-word barrier to justice

Ivo Kuka, too, fled his home after he was imprisoned
and tortured as a political prisoner in Cameroon due
to his membership of the SCNC. Ivo was arrested
after attending an SCNC demonstration and detained
for five days, during which he was tortured - hung
upside down, beaten on the soles of his feet, and
beaten in the face for which he received stitches -
and sexually assaulted. As Robert and Ivo found,
sanctuary was to be hard to find. While the worst
excesses of violence and mistreatment may have
been left behind in Cameroon, in the UK Ivo found
striking similarities: once again, imprisoned and
denied the right to a fair trial. The UK government
refused to listen to Ivo's story and fought to send him
back to face more of the same treatment. In Ivo's
own words, they signed his death warrant.

On arrival in the UK, Ivo was imprisoned in
Harmondsworth detention centre, near Heathrow.
Central to the miscarriage of justice Ivo was
subjected to was his placement in the 'detained fast-
track' (DFT) process. DFT has been described by
campaign group Detention Action as "...*structured to
the maximum disadvantage of asylum-seekers at
every stage. Conditions and timescales operate to
make it impossible for many asylum-seekers to*

understand or actively engage with the asylum process.[2]

The premise of DFT is to process asylum claims as fast as possible and individuals placed in the process are detained while their claim is decided - the period from interview to decision is often a matter of days. The UKBA now has a target of processing 30 per cent of claims through the fast track procedure. While there has been a steep decline in asylum applications in recent years, allocation to the fast track has increased from 1,672 in 2008 to 2,571 in 2010.The process has been under intense criticism and legal challenges, both because of its use of administrative detention and because the speed represents such a significant barrier to justice that a positive outcome almost impossible.

According to the government's own guidelines, Ivo should not have been included on the DFT process because he was a victim of torture. Including rape and torture victims in the process has drawn the UKBA severe criticism from the UN, but the practice continues[3].

The story of Ivo Kuka

"When I booked for an appointment to claim asylum, never did I know that I was to be detained and treated as a criminal. On the 19th of October 2012,

---

2   *Fast Track to Despair,* Detention Action, May 2011 p.3, http://www.irr.org.uk/pdf2/FastTracktoDespair.pdf
3   'UK detention of torture victims "inhumane"', *Guardian,* 23 February 2012, http://www.theguardian.com/uk/2012/feb/23/uk-detention-torture-victims-inhumane

10:45 am, I arrived in Croydon for my asylum claim. I was received by a lady and taken in to a single room.

"She said she was going to conduct my screening interview and I was OK with that? The interview was conducted. At the end she told me it was decided to put my case on 'fast track'. Not knowing what it meant I said that was OK. Later in the evening I was taken downstairs and handed over to some officers who searched me and locked me up in a room, taking my phone away from me. This act raised some concern in me and I asked if something was wrong. The only answer I got was a small piece of paper with an address on it.

"The address was Harmondsworth's. Late in the night three of us were taken into a van and driven to Harmondsworth. When I got up the following morning I could not believe what was going on. I said to myself, 'I am in prison'. I was traumatised, depressed and scared, but as a man I put on the helmet of courage and started to do what I saw others do. I began to ask my new friends what 'fast track' was and from the different explanations, I knew I was in a difficult situation, and not alone. I came to discover that asylum seekers detained in the fast track have very limited time and resources to present their case, or to prepare for any appeal, if you have the chance at all to be allowed to appeal while in the UK.

"The procedures under the detained fast track show that from the day you claim asylum you have just nine days for your claim to be decided upon. It states: 'From Day 9 it may be possible to have your appeal reconsidered by the asylum immigration tribunal but this is not guaranteed.' You can find yourself detained for years without your case being decided upon and you are still in the fast track system, treated like a criminal. If you complain about the food you will be sent to the 'F-wing', a wing specially made for psychological torture. You are with three people in a room and the toilet is in the same room, openly and just right next to you.

"I came across one guy who has been here for one year and three months. He narrated his story to me, like we were already friends. The second time we were talking about our stories I came to discover that what he said to me the first time was slightly different from what he was telling me now. I decided to have a close look at all his paperwork from the Home Office. He has been interviewed many times and he was showing high levels of traumatic stress.

"In his application, the peripheral details of the account are more likely to be inconsistent than the recall of details that are central to the account. I am pleading for him with the authorities and case owner that such inconsistencies should not be relied on as indicating the lack of credibility. Tell me, if one is not well-trained to handle such information how can an asylum claim be well managed?

"In the DFT case owners lay excessive and inappropriate emphasis on factors that are not in any way to be considered relevant to the credibility assessment. They place a very heavy burden on us, demanding us to prove our claims in a very short period of time. In my case I had a substantive interview on the 24th October and I told my case owner I could provide evidence from Cameroon. To my greatest dismay, I was served a refusal letter the following day. I had less than 24 hours to provide evidence from Cameroon. In these 24 hours, I also had to send the documentation to my solicitor, who has to look for and send the documents to an expert to verify the authenticity, and send them back to the solicitor before they could be handed over to the case owner. This truly is 'fast track'. Even so, when you manage to produce the evidence, the case owners - who are the decision makers - fail to pursue and evaluate the evidence.

"I have been a subject to torture, sexual assault and other acts of serious violence. On my arrival at the removal centre I was supposed to receive the necessary medical and psychological treatment, but instead I am tortured psychologically in detention. Each time you complain about an illness you are given two tablets of paracetamol. I requested rule 35 [evidence that detainees are particularly vulnerable, for example have been victims of torture, or whose physical or mental health is likely to suffer as a result of detention] from the health care to use as evidence for my claim. It took weeks to come.

"Solicitors also play a very significant role in the DFT. In my case, I met with my solicitor for the first time just a few minutes before my substantive interview. We had to talk just for about five minutes before my interview started. The solicitor had no knowledge of my case. After my refusal letter had been served, I was given the right to appeal within two days. My solicitor told me on the last day, just a few hours before the deadline, to do it by myself and that she could not file the appeal for me.

"I learned that in Germany when you seek asylum you will be given a residence permit for specific purposes, which allow you to stay in the country legally until your asylum procedure is completed. This also is seen in many other European countries, but in the UK when you seek asylum, you are imprisoned. Asylum seeking has turned to be a serious crime in the UK. I served a long-term prison sentence in Cameroon for belonging to SCNC and in the UK I am serving another undetermined prison term for seeking asylum. Where are the human rights?"

Since sharing his story with Refugee Radio, Ivo was thankfully released. On his third appearance in court, and after four months in detention, a judge finally found in favour of his appeal and he was granted refugee status. The judge indicated that Ivo's outspoken approach about the situation in Cameroon and his treatment in the UK, including his testimony in the Refugee Radio magazine, had helped his case.

Ivo is now studying health and social care management and doing voluntary work. He has not stopped campaigning for Southern Cameroon: "The struggle we will not let go. We're still fighting for independence. We won't let that go so easily." He is part of a group which comes together every three months to talk about how to advance the cause through British politics.

Since release, he has spoken out about detention and the fast-track process to mainstream news such as the BBC and ITV. "There should be an alternative method to immigration detention. Cases should be treated in the community," he says, "The fast-track process shouldn't even exist. It should be abolished."

Robert, at the time of writing, is still living in limbo, housed in temporary accommodation and waiting for a decision on his claim. For him, the question remains unanswered: Where are the human rights?

Stories of Trauma and Strength: Refugee Radio's Resilience Panel

Nina Yeo

In 2012, Refugee Radio started a project called the Resilience Panel, a supportive, participatory volunteering opportunity for refugees and migrants who have experienced trauma.

In essence, the project – for which I have worked as Group Facilitator - is about recognising and building resilience, by acknowledging the strength and skills that participants possess. Resilience not only aids recovery from previous experiences, but also increases our ability to withstand future adversity. The Resilience Panel provides participants with the opportunity to reflect on the challenges they have faced in their lives, coping strategies which have been useful to overcome them, and how things could be changed for the better.

Individuals are referred to the Panel from mental health services, community groups and via word of mouth, and come together to discuss their experiences and ideas. The group then finds a way to share their knowledge with the wider community, through advocacy and practical workshops. Workshops given by the 2012 and 2013 groups have involved participatory sessions with young refugees, refugee women's groups, members of an English project for migrants, and at an International Women's Day event.

There is a great need for mental health support for refugees and asylum seekers, and throughout the project we found several recurring themes that I've illustrated below with examples. The examples are drawn from the stories of Panel members but with names and details changed to protect anonymity. The themes we discussed collectively during the projects of the last two years included the impact of the asylum process itself on people who've already experienced trauma, the difficulties people have in accessing services, and the situations people find themselves in in the UK.

But to start with, what do we mean by 'trauma'? The dictionary definition is 'a wound or injury', 'an emotional shock' or 'the state or condition caused by a physical or emotional shock'. It's a common phenomenon, for example when faced with the unexpected death of a loved one, or the loss of possessions. When adequate social and financial support structures are in place, people are often able to mourn for and repair from this loss, and the traumatised state of 'shock' may be short-lived.

However, many instances of trauma may take longer to recuperate from. Events such as violent crimes, for example, and acts of corruption from those in positions of power may threaten our sense of safety and justice. When such trauma occurs it can leave lasting effects known as post-traumatic stress symptoms, and the condition PTSD (post-traumatic stress disorder). These symptoms include flashbacks and intrusive memories or 're-experiencing', contrasted with amnesia and avoidance of stimuli which serve as reminders of the trauma.[1] Other symptoms include nightmares and disturbed sleep, hypervigilance, emotional numbing, a sense of detachment, and accompanying anxiety and depression.[2] Strong feelings of fear, anger, sadness and desperation may be compounded by survivor guilt - the sense that they did not deserve to survive, particularly when friends or family have perished.[3] Some survivors may even feel they have been contaminated by evil, as their perpetrators have become mentally internalised during traumatic events.[4] This may exacerbate feelings of worthlessness.

---

1   World Health Organisation, *International Classification of Diseases (ICD) Version 10 Online Version F43.1* http://apps.who.int/classifications/icd10/browse/2010/en#/F40-F48 accessed 16.02.2014.
2   Ibid.
3   Blackwell, D. (2013) 'States of terror and terrorist states: oppression and liberation in political and therapeutic contexts' *in Terror Within and Without; Attachment and Disintegration: Clinical Work on the Edge* (Judy Yellin and Orit Badouk Epstein eds.) Karnac, London. p.63.
4   Sachs, A. (2012) 'Intergenerational Transmission of Massive Trauma' in *Terror Within and Without*, ibid, p.30.

        Refugees are defined by the United Nations
High Commissioner for Refugees (UNHCR) as people
outside their country of origin due to a well-founded
fear of persecution.[5] Therefore, it is a given that
many refugees worldwide will have gone through
traumatic experiences.[6]

Can you hear me?

The process of applying for asylum, which many
Resilience Panel participants had experienced,
involves telling their story of survival and trauma.
Therefore, a common thread of discussion was the
significance asylum seekers and refugees'
testimonies held in shaping their experiences in the
UK.
        When people apply for asylum, their account of
events is considered alongside other information to
determine whether or not it meets the 'refugee'
definition. The outcome is based on narrow criteria,
in a system designed primarily to protect UK borders,
rather than those who seek safety. However, it may
signify far more than this to the teller of the tale. A
stamp of approval implies legitimacy - that the story
is believed. Being given refugee status, with related
rights and opportunities, confirms the perceived
worth of the applicant.
        Yet the conditions in which the asylum
applicant tells their tale, on which so much rests, are
likely to be far from ideal. Most encounter the

---

5   World Health Organisation, *ICD 10 F43.1.*
6   United Nations High Commissioner for Refugees, *UNHCR Mid
Year Trends 2013*, UHNCR Website
http://www.unhcr.org/52af08d26.html accessed 17/02/2014.

complex process, in an unfamiliar language, within the first few hours of arrival in the UK, after fleeing from a situation of extreme stress. There may also be cultural factors which prevent asylum seekers from giving an accurate account of incidents such as sexual violence, disclosure of which may have led to disrespect or even punishment in some countries. In addition to this, the person may be experiencing post-traumatic stress symptoms, including absent or intrusive memories. Under such conditions, it is not surprising that first testimonies may display some inconsistencies or omit important details.

When these errors are used as proof that their account was inaccurate or false, this can cause people a great deal more suffering. An unsuccessful asylum case was commonly reported to increase refugees' own feelings of self-doubt, guilt and worthlessness. As a consequence, many refugee participants of the Resilience Panel felt that the trauma they experienced consisted not only of events in their home countries and their flight to the UK, but also the process of applying for asylum.

There is also a danger with the asylum process that, because a successful asylum claim is one that emphasises the individual's vulnerability, claiming asylum is inherently more disempowering than empowering. To focus solely on the traumatic nature of refugee stories is to omit the wealth of their other life experiences, and the strength they have developed in order to survive. Asylum seekers' strengths may be played upon against their favour: any fortunate aspects of their case, however small, may help form an argument against granting asylum. This focus on extreme vulnerability is often at odds with the fighting spirit of those who have endured lengthy and dangerous journeys to reach the UK. It also undermines attempts to rebuild lives following traumatic experiences.

One of the first tasks of Resilience Panel groups was to create an atmosphere of safety, where participants were able to share some of their life experiences, if they chose to. Owning and validating testimonies with those who have had similar experiences can help to lessen the sense of guilt and blame many asylum seekers direct at themselves. This may enable them to separate the strong feelings attached to what they have experienced from the legal process of seeking asylum. Otherwise, harsh judgements of others may yet again be internalised.

Halka

Halka walked across the Saharan desert to get to the UK when he was 14 years old. His father was a member of a rebel organisation who were at civil war with the government in his home country. The family were preparing to have dinner one night when members of the national army entered the house and shot his father dead, while Halka remained unseen in the pantry. Shortly afterwards, he left the country with his older brother as their lives were also in danger. However, his brother was recruited by militia on the way, leaving Halka to finish his arduous journey alone.

When Halka arrived in the UK he made a claim for asylum. As he spoke no English, he was provided with an interpreter. The interpreter was a speaker of his native language, Arabic, but originated from a different country and spoke a different dialect. Terrified of the uniformed officials who questioned him, and grateful to have been provided an aid with whom he could make himself partially understood, it did not occur to Halka to question this. In his asylum statement, the party responsible for murdering his father was recorded as the rebel group, rather than the ruling government. Halka's asylum claim was refused, as the UK Border Agency claimed that the threat from the rebel organisation recorded as responsible for his father's death was now diminished. However, as he was an unaccompanied minor he was granted temporary leave to remain in the UK until the age of 17. Halka did not understand the full relevance of this, but was relieved to be told that for the time being he could stay in the UK.

Halka was placed with a foster family of the same nationality as himself, and attended college where he enrolled on a language course. He was a dedicated student and soon became fluent in English. He enjoyed playing basketball and joined the college team. Most importantly, Halka got on very well with his foster parents, who he called mother and father. He came to realise that his family life at home had been very difficult, as his biological father had been a harsh and authoritarian parent. A couple of years later, Halka's social worker explained he would soon have to leave his foster family, and reapply for asylum as he was now 17 and his leave to remain in the UK was about to expire. Halka was devastated, as he had

*not been aware of his insecure legal status. He did
not want to leave the family he had come to think of
as his own, and could not imagine returning to his
country of origin, where he believed his life would
still be in danger. Accompanied by a support worker,
Halka sought advice from a refugee advice agency.
He explained that the details of his case had been
recorded incorrectly as the interpreter had not
understood him fully.*

*The adviser became frustrated after looking at
his papers. 'Why didn't you refute the statement at
the time?' she questioned Halka angrily. 'If you
change your story now, you will lack credibility. Your
level of English is now excellent, so no judge will
believe you didn't understand. You've messed this up
and there is nothing that can be done.' Halka burst
into tears. 'How would I know that I could challenge
the statement, when I was a child and I was so
frightened?' he asked the support worker, who tried
to comfort him, on the way back. 'I was in an
unfamiliar place and everyone spoke a language I
didn't understand. I didn't want to make any trouble.
I have worked so hard to learn English and fit in
here. But now I feel that everything I've done is
wrong. It's all my fault'.*

Asking for help

Another recurring theme for Resilience Panel
sessions was the difficulty participants experienced
in asking for assistance from health services. Despite
the prevalence of mental health problems in the
refugee population, asking for help to recover from

traumatic experiences was particularly problematic. Common barriers included language and cultural differences, a lack of awareness of services, difficulty in trusting others and a sense of not deserving help. Some people lacked confidence in explaining their symptoms to GPs and other health professionals, and feared they would be met with a harsh reaction.

Regret over their perceived actions at the time, a sense of disbelief or unreality in relation to events, and the sense (often compounded by cultural differences) that they could not be talked about, were common experiences of panel members. When seeking assistance from mental health services traumatised refugees can feel they are being asked - yet again - to offer their story up for judgement against a set of criteria. As when they sought asylum, refugees may once again experience fear and uncertainty about whether they would be believed, how much of events they could bear to tell to a stranger, and how to describe their symptoms. Some Resilience Panel participants reported feeling rejected and worthless if they were found not to meet the criteria for services, or if, as was more common, they were unavailable or subject to long waiting times due to high demand and scarce resources.

Depending on the severity and length of time of post-traumatic stress reactions, refugees and other survivors of trauma who are referred to mental health services may be given a diagnosis of PTSD, and offered specialist help. The National Institute for Health and Care Excellence (NICE) guidelines for PTSD indicate individuals with symptoms lasting longer than four weeks, or with severe symptoms, should be offered trauma-focused psychological treatment such as cognitive behavioural therapy or EMDR (eye movement desensitisation and reprocessing).[7]

Some participants accessing trauma-focused short-term treatments found them of great benefit but felt a longer intervention was necessary, given the magnitude of their traumatic experiences. This was often not on offer, or required a request for re-referral via their GP followed by another period of waiting, which could be a frustrating and lengthy process. However, specialist trauma treatments were not always on offer. Individuals accessing more mainstream services sometimes experienced a lack of clarity about what they could expect from them, leading to misunderstanding and a sense of suspicion. When there was an awareness of refugees' situations, explanations were given and boundaries were made clear, this was reassuring and enabled participants to access the help they needed. Others found accessing community organisations, alternative therapies, sports and relaxation more beneficial.

The panel devised a leaflet about post-traumatic stress symptoms, which refugees could use when attempting to access services. Panel members also wrote a role play which they performed during workshop sessions with the wider community, to help other refugees and migrants to gain confidence. The role play is summarised below.

---

7   National Institute for Health and Care Excellence, Clinical Guideline 26 issued March 2005: Post-Traumatic Stress Disorder (PTSD): The management of PTSD in children and adults in primary and secondary care.

Dina

*Dina went to the GP because she was experiencing
terrible nightmares. Male residents of her
accommodation were making a lot of noise during the
evenings, which triggered frightening memories of
being held in an army barracks in her country of
origin. The first doctor she saw was dismissive, and
told her to make a warm drink at night and have a
bath before going to bed. Two weeks later, Dina
returned to see a female doctor, bringing a leaflet
about PTSD with her. This time she was able to be
more open about her experiences and how much they
were affecting her. She was referred to see a
counsellor for an assessment. Dina had never heard
of a counsellor before and was not aware of the
boundaries to their role. She brought her housing
papers to the assessment, in the hope that the
counsellor would be able to help her move
accommodation. The counsellor told her that she
could not help her with things like that, without
explaining why.*

*Dina was upset after the session as she felt that
the counsellor didn't like her, or thought that she did
not deserve help. She was uncertain about returning
for her next appointment. However, with a friend's
encouragement she decided to return, and found that
she had been assigned to a different counsellor. The
new counsellor spent time at the beginning
explaining to her that counselling was about
exploring past experiences and difficult feelings. She
said that she would not be able to give Dina practical*

help, although she could try to point her in the right direction. Dina went home feeling reassured and looked forward to being able to see the counsellor again. She was now ready to speak to the counsellor more openly about what was troubling her.

Disempowered by the system

Resilience panel members spoke of the numerous ways in which just being an 'asylum seeker' undermined their power. Prohibiting asylum seekers from working increased their sense of helplessness, and they could lose faith in their abilities. Welfare payments for asylum seekers are substantially less than Jobseekers Allowance rates, placing vulnerable individuals well below the poverty line.[8]

Panel members who required housing while seeking asylum were accommodated under the national dispersal system. Implemented in 1999, this scheme moves asylum seekers out of the south-east and into areas with cheaper accommodation, which by their very nature tend to be areas of economic deprivation and social problems. Hostility towards asylum seekers in the UK may be felt by those who are themselves victims of the welfare system - when caught up in lengthy battles for housing and benefits, refugees may be seen as competitors, an easier target to blame than the system which they rely upon to survive. The national dispersal policy has, in fact, conveniently encouraged negative feeling towards

---

8   UK Government, 'Asylum Support', UK Government website https://www.gov.uk/asylum-support/what-youll-get accessed 02/03/2014.

asylum seekers, by ensuring that the communities who host them those with the least socio-economic and emotional resources themselves. Additional funding to establish support structures and housing for refugees in dispersal areas was granted initially, before being scaled back.[9]

Panel members reported very poor housing conditions, no choice of destination and being moved unexpectedly, making it difficult to establish support networks or a sense of belonging. 'Section 4', a limited form of support available to asylum seekers with rejected asylum claims, provided further reduced payments and housing options, leading to increased hardship and a sense of worthlessness. Finally, many asylum claimants had spent lengthy periods of time waiting for the outcome of their asylum cases, amid uncertainty and fears about having to return to their countries of origin. This situation intensified post-traumatic stress symptoms, and made recovery and positive action difficult.

Majid

Majid came to the UK in the 1980s after being involved in political activities in the Middle Eastern country he originated from. He left quickly without saying goodbye to his wife and children, for fear of putting their lives in danger. He comforted himself

---

9   Institute of Race Relations (IRR), 'Public Spending Cuts Savage Dispersal System' ,27/01/2011, IRR website http://www.irr.org.uk/news/public-spending-cuts-savage-dispersal-system/ accessed 22/02/2014.

with the fact that as soon as he was granted asylum, he would send for his family and they would be reunited. Majid claimed asylum and settled in Middlesbrough, where he had a friend. His temporary status document entitled him to work, and he found employment in the material industry. However, after waiting for several years, he had heard nothing back from the Home Office in relation to his asylum claim. Majid believed his solicitor may be at fault, and changed legal provider. However, he still heard nothing.

Then, due to an economic downturn in the area, Majid's company went bankrupt and he went to the job centre to look for further employment. However, as conditions had now changed for asylum seekers, Majid was told that his immigration document was no longer valid and therefore he was not entitled to work. Shortly afterwards, he was forced to leave his accommodation and his entitlement to benefits was withdrawn. After several months of relying on the goodwill of friends to accommodate him and provide him with food, he was forced to apply for Section 4. This very limited form of support did not provide any money, but entitled him to food vouchers and accommodation which could be anywhere in the UK. He was moved at very short notice to Plymouth, and was only allowed to take one suitcase. As Plymouth was on the other side of the country from Middlesbrough and was an expensive journey, he was unable to return to visit friends or collect any of his other possessions. This meant he had no kitchen utensils and no money to purchase any. He could only spend his vouchers in supermarkets. In the Section 4 accommodation, Majid had to share a room with two *other men, including one who chain smoked in his bed and another who was haunted by nightmares of being tortured and howled in his sleep most nights.*

Although Majid was still in telephone contact with his wife and children, they expressed some hostility towards him. Majid knew that they blamed him for not being able to gain asylum status and bring them to the UK, believing he was living in luxury here without sending money home. Twenty years had now passed since Majid had arrived in the UK, and his wife no longer trusted him. She accused him of lying about his status to keep her and the children away, because he had taken another lover. This could not be further from the truth, as Majid was racked with guilt about having abandoned his family. As he had waited so long for an outcome to his asylum claim, and his situation had got worse and worse, he gave up hope of ever finding a resolution. He had lost touch with his solicitor in Middlesbrough, and had no money to return there or make phone calls. However, he attended a drop-in session at a local community centre and was advised to write to his MP about his situation. The MP contacted the Home Office on his behalf and within a fortnight, he received a letter granting him leave to remain, due to the fact that he had been here for over 14 years. Majid could not believe it. 'Half my life has been spent waiting for an answer. Then someone very important writes a letter, and the response comes straight away. It was all about power, and I had none.'

Recurring problems and negative decisions

As members of the Panel could testify, failed asylum seekers find themselves in horrendously difficult circumstances. Many cannot return to their country of origin because they are stateless, or because returns are considered too dangerous due to conflict. Others fear for their lives if they do so, and do not see returning as a viable option.

Migrants who have come to the UK for work or study purposes, but are later affected by illness or other adverse circumstances, are another group of people with very few rights. Irregular migrants seeking to escape from poverty or access life-saving healthcare may be faced with even more limited choices. The state has the capacity to detain up to 3,725 asylum seekers, failed asylum seekers and migrants with insecure immigration status, indefinitely in immigration detention in the UK; there are also short-term holdings for a further 89 individuals, and 44 families.[10] There are also a significant number of individuals living in destitution in the UK, with no recourse to public funds and no right to work. Although this forgotten, hidden group of people is by definition hard to quantify, a 2009

---

10   Refugee Council, *Refugee Council Information; Detention in the Asylum System; April 2013*, p.1.
http://www.refugeecouncil.org.uk/assets/0002/7333/130326Detention_i
n_the_Asylum_System.pdf (accessed 19/02/2014).

estimate suggests there may be up to 500,000 failed asylum seekers living underground.[11]

Frequently branded as 'illegal', bogus claimants by the general public and the press, destitute migrants and asylum seekers have no choice but to rely on handouts from religious groups and charities or dangerous, poorly paid work on the black market. Section 21 of the *National Assistance Act 1948* gives local authorities a duty to house, 'those who by reasons of age, illness or disability or any other circumstances are in need of care and attention which is not otherwise available to them'.[12] In practice, the cover provided by the legislation is very limited. Migrants and failed asylum seekers, who are subject to the *Immigration and Asylum Act 1999*, may not claim under this act if their needs arise solely as a result of destitution and the related impact on health.[13] Once again, the provision both emphasises the vulnerability of the applicant rather than their resilience, and operates on exclusive criteria.

Being in a powerless situation may compromise not only how we feel in our minds, but also in our bodies. If we return to the definition of trauma at the beginning of this chapter, we see that the same word serves to mean a physical or emotional wound, and a

---

11   British Red Cross, 'Not gone, but forgotten; The urgent need for a more humane asylum system', p.7. http://www.redcross.org.uk/About-us/Advocacy/~/media/BritishRedCross/Documents/About%20us/Not%20gone%20but%20forgotten%20destitution%20report.pdf (accessed 19/02/2014)
12   Great Britain, National Assistance Act 1948: Elizabeth II. Section 21. (1948) London: The Stationery Office.
13   Ibid.

physical or emotional shock as the result of this wound. Psychosomatic reactions, in which there is no biological cause for physical pain, are common among refugee survivors.[14] Afflictions can be a mask for emotional pain, or felt in an area of the body involved in original traumatic incidents, as a form of re-experiencing.[15] However, chronic physical health conditions with biological origins may also be more common in this group of people than in the general population. A study of physical and mental health in 178 refugees and 232 asylum seekers in reception centres in the Netherlands found that 59 per cent of asylum seekers and 42 per cent of refugees considered their health to be poor in general.[16] Co-morbidity was also high, with over half of respondents diagnosed with more than one chronic condition.

Interestingly, rates of post-traumatic stress, anxiety and depression were higher amongst asylum seekers than refugees, showing a correlation between mental wellbeing and legal status. Having a sense of purpose and hope for the future has a meaningful impact on our health. Public Health Specialist Claire Mitchison's article in *Happiness: Brighton and Hove 2012-13 Public Health Report*, cited being unable to work due to a disability or health problem to be the biggest risk factor for

---

14   Alayarian, A. (2007) 'My experience of clinical work with refugees and asylum seekers' in *Resilience, Suffering, and Creativity*. Karnac, London, p.145.
15   Ibid.
16   Annette A. M. Gerritsen et al. (2006). 'The physical and mental health of Afghan, Iranian and Somali asylum seekers and refugees living in the Netherlands' in *Social Psychiatry Psychiatric Epidemiology*. 41: 18-26.

developing depression.[17] Refugees can find
themselves in a similar position, as aside from being
unable to work while seeking asylum, they may
struggle to find work even once granted status due to
the language barrier and their qualifications not
being recognised.

Public Health Consultant Max Kammerling
quotes a recent report from the Harvard School of
Public Health, which finds that, 'Serious, sustained
stress or fear can alter biological systems in a way
that, over time, adds up to wear and tear and,
eventually, illnesses such as heart disease, stroke,
and diabetes'.[18] Kammerling goes on to suggest that,
'Feelings of a lack of control over life may account for
more than half the mortality risk for people of low
social status'.[19]

It is not surprising, therefore, that the
traumatic experiences refugees suffer, coupled with
years of uncertain status and limited opportunities
may lead to poor physical and mental health.

---

17   Mitchison, C. 'Depression' in *Happiness; The Eternal Pursuit;
Annual Report of the Director of Public Health Brighton and Hove
2012/2013*, p 12. http://www.brighton-
hove.gov.uk/sites/brightonhove.gov.uk/files/Director%20of%20Public%
20Health%20Annual%20Report%202013_web_0.pdf (accessed
19/02/2014)
18   Kammerling, M. 'The case for happiness' in *Happiness; The
Eternal Pursuit; Annual Report of the Director of Public Health
Brighton and Hove 2012/2013*,p.4.
19   Ibid.

Japinda

Japinda came to the UK to work as a dental nurse for a firm in Bristol, having held a similar position in her native South Asian country. She earned enough to send a significant sum home to support her brothers and sisters, while living comfortably in a shared house with friends. She had been working there for several years and had developed strong links with the community in Bristol, where she felt settled. Then at the age of 33, Japinda became ill. She was diagnosed with a chronic illness which required regular treatment if it was not to become progressive. After being granted some sick leave, Japinda was required to return to work but unfortunately was unable to complete all of her duties due to her poor health. After a lengthy tribunal process, capability proceedings were brought against Japinda and she lost her job. This meant her employment visa was no longer valid. Japinda was aware that the state health services in her country of origin were poor, and that she would not be able to afford the private medical treatment she needed. Faced with the prospect of returning home and fearing she was still too unwell to work, Japinda felt as if a death sentence hung over her. She began to have terrifying nightmares, and was unable to sleep. She lost her appetite and could no longer find pleasure in all the things she had previously enjoyed. After seeking advice from a voluntary organisation, Japinda made a claim under Section 21. However, her claim was overturned because it was deemed that her physical health was not poor enough. When she described the torment she was suffering, it was suggested to her that she make a claim under her mental health instead. Japinda could not believe that the court could not see that physical health, mental wellbeing and legal status were all interlinked. 'How can I feel well in my mind, knowing that I must return to a country where my physical health will deteriorate? How can I recover physically when I am not well in my mind? I am not a health tourist. I came here to work, not to be sick. Now I feel as if I make myself into a complete victim, because the more helpless and sicker I am, the more likely it is that I can stay.'

Scope

Even when they were not able to work, engaging in meaningful activities in connection with other people was found by the Resilience Panel to be the best healer for trauma. Many participants found that concentrating on taking care of themselves was an important first step which improved both their physically and mental health, and promoted a sense of self-worth. Walking, yoga, cooking healthy food together and accessing low cost alternative therapies were all of benefit.

Once relative wellbeing had been achieved, dedication to political activism, study, meditation or helping others offered a renewed set of shared values and experiences. Both establishing self-care skills and finding a sense of purpose enabled participants to establish an identity in which they were not merely passive recipients of help, as they may perceive themselves to be within the asylum, social welfare and mental health systems. Facilitating

communication with other asylum seekers and
migrants, politicians and service providers is to move
in the right direction to make positive changes to
these systems, albeit in the face of widespread cuts.
Successes of Resilience Panel members to date have
included writing to a local MP, and organising a
health conference with speakers from the NHS and
the voluntary sector.

     Standing up for what we believe in has
restorative power, even when few resources are
available.

They'll heal in time, you said,
The wounds that ran so deep
They scratched the surface of the earth when we
walked on it.

After the lights of autumn,
Our hollows fill with rain, and run clear.

But will there be time,
When we are whole enough to start as new?
In the midst of not knowing, we set sail.

Visible Community: Hidden Identities

Gharghasht

The experience of identity crisis, and being lost in a new environment that is very different from your roots, is something Afghans tend to keep private and deal with in an Afghan way. Hardly any research has been done about this issue within our communities. I decided to investigate this theme, looking at what others have said and written, and also doing my own research. I put the question of how Afghans identify themselves in different societies to people I know. The main responses came from Afghan women - there seems to be a need among women to discuss this issue. I also explain some of my own thoughts as an Afghan man about what I've experienced myself, both living in the UK and running 'Afghan Voice Radio'. But before I start, I think it is important to explain what – for me - it means to be an Afghan.

Afghan Identity

This is a question that can only be raised when you live outside Afghanistan. In Afghanistan life is a routine. Everything is in place: Azaan (the call to prayer), life on the streets, morning bakeries, walks to school or work, and chai being served everywhere. Being Afghan is just everyday life, as I suppose it is for British people in the Britain. Time is regulated by the moon and by prayers, by nature. In the West time regulates life, which is in its turn regulated by the economy: you have to be somewhere on time, or start something at a certain time and end it before a deadline. This difference is probably the reason why a lot of Afghans are always late. Even on a boring, rainy day, I will be late.

In Britain people contribute by making money for the economy. You aim to make enough money to support yourself, your own career, your own life. It is a very individualistic society, where your own choices and your own life come first and your family comes second, third, or even fourth. In Afghanistan the focus is on contributing to society and your family. Contributing to society can be in many ways not necessarily related to money, but more to country and community life. Your choices in life, the 'dos and don'ts', are made by your family. In liberal families you have a voice and choice, but it is important to have your parents' blessings in whatever you decide, because your future is also their future and old age. As an Afghan your choices create a reflection within your or your family's community, and will have an impact on both your own and their life, no matter where you are in the world.

Afghans have a laid back attitude towards destiny - when it's your time, it's your time. Allah knows best and our thoughts and conversation are punctuated by a lot of 'InshAllahs'. This laid-back attitude can put us in unnecessary danger, but it also gives us the strength and flexibility to survive in the most absurd situations and adjust ourselves to the world around us. Afghans are eager learners and love to learn new things and explore the world as soon as they get the opportunity.

This might give the impression that Afghans have no problem adjusting at all, but it would not be Afghan unless it were a little bit more complicated. Afghanistan is a country of many ethnicities, culturally rooted within their own ethnic tribal structure. But cross-tribal marriages and other irregularities are on the increase and this can erode traditional assumptions about identity, even among Afghans in Afghanistan. Sometimes an identity crisis is necessary for development. It is as if Afghans can be too stubborn to accept that cultural values and traditions are fluid, and things which develop. Afghans have the tendency to cling to their roots and, to be honest, so do I. However much I might love to explore the world and learn new things, Afghanistan remains in my heart and in my soul.

For me being an Afghan means living according to my tribal codes, in my case Pashtunwali, but with a liberal mindset towards others: "Live and let live." I see all cultures as impressive and beautiful. These cultural codes define my identity and are embedded within a rich cultural history, they run in my veins, in my blood. Ignoring these codes would amount to ignoring my very being, so it is important for me to keep them alive. The problem is that life in the UK is not designed for everyone to live fully according to their own cultural codes. The solution is to balance and compromise, to integrate, but never assimilate. You combine your own culture with the reality of the outside world around you. For this reason I practice my Pashtunwali inside the privacy of my own home and when I go outside I adjust myself to the society around me. "You can take the Pathan out of the Pashtunwali, but you never can take the Pashtunwali out of the Pathan."

There's another thing about identity which is important to mention but frequently gets forgotten. Although the vast majority of Afghans are Muslim, Afghans are diverse as any other human being, in gender, ethnicity, background and faith. There are Afghan Sikh communities, Hindus, Jews, Christians, Buddhists, Atheists and of course there are the blow-yourself-up extremists, conservatives, liberals, 'Ramadan Muslims', part-time Muslims, full-time Muslims and occasional Muslims.

A different country.

The stories of the Afghan diaspora are not new; these stories exist from fleeing more than thirty years of war and conflict. There are around five million Afghans living all around the world and Afghans have been building communities in new countries for a long time. Children have been born and raised in different countries, from the refugee camps in Pakistan to as far away as the U.S., Australia and Europe. But the undeniable fact about being Afghan is that wherever we are in the world, we know each other. This is due to our tribal roots. It is the curse and the blessing of being an Afghan.

Waking up in the morning in a new country does not make you change your identity. However, the things that happen to you in the new country will make change the way you feel about yourself, your culture and the world around you. And these feelings can lead to questions about who you are, what are you developing into?

Dr Esmael Darman is a well-known Afghan clinical psychologist and creator of the first online website on psychology and mental health for Afghanistan (Rawan Online) and he has an impressive track record as a specialist in Afghanistan. Dr Darman currently lives in the U.S., and points out that there are several factors relating to a feeling of identity crisis with the Afghan community and the diaspora.

First of all, Afghan migration has not been planned like that of many other nationalities. People left the country because they had to. Coming to a new country against your wishes and without a plan creates a feeling of resistance to change. Secondly, there is the difference between the values of collectivistic Afghan society and those of individualistic Western society. In a collectivist society you're controlled by groups (and shaming, group honour). In Afghan families abroad, many parents maintain those values. However their children, faced by two different cultures, start living a double life to maintain cultural pride on the one hand, and deal with peer pressure on the other. This approach brings with it a tremendous amount of emotional and cognitive dissonance. Finally, there is the fact that whatever our family or community codes, we as Afghans we have never formed a strong "national identity". Add to these factors the trauma of conflict, low education levels, language barriers, lack of interest in getting to know a new culture, and strict religious/traditional values, and you come up with a combination of factors that impedes integration and assimilation.

Nushin Arbabzadah is an Afghan journalist and cultural critic who was raised in Afghanistan and educated in Europe. She worked for the BBC before moving to Los Angeles, where she teaches courses on Middle Eastern media at UCLA. She is the author of several books, including "Afghan Rumour Bazaar": Secret Sub-Cultures, Hidden Worlds and the Everyday Life of the Absurd. In part of her book she explains how her migration from Afghanistan changed her from a typical Afghan girl who kept her gaze fixed to the ground and her mouth shut, into a vocal, educated and self-confident woman. She found that her female Afghan quality of submissive shyness was not only useless in Europe, but also guaranteed a life spent in poverty. In Europe an economically productive society requires both men and women to work hard to keep the country going. But not all girls respond to the culture clash as Nushin did. "The girls I knew in Germany developed anorexia and bulimia and became experts in leading double lives," she says. Afghans live all over the world, including some who've made it into Hollywood. Fahim Fazli and Sitara Attaie are two Afghan actors who have established a career in the U.S. Their passion and talent for acting, their motivation and energy, their

Afghan stubbornness and never-give-up attitude has taken them to levels that many British or American actors can only dream of. But they do experience being typecast most of the time, and they've learned that the golden rules of Hollywood are not to talk about politics or religion if you pursue a career.

Talking to Afghan Voice Radio, Fahim Fazli described himself as an Afghan American actor, writer and cultural adviser. He loves both countries and even seems to feel patriotism for both, with an attitude of accepting the culture where you live. If you criticize it, or clearly dislike it, you can always leave. He is thankful that the U.S. gave him a home and a chance to realize his dream. He does not mind being typecast as a villain or terrorist, he says, since this gives him roles in blockbuster films. He actively promotes and encourages Afghan actors to come to Hollywood and is trying to improve Hollywood's knowledge and understanding of Afghan culture. Fahim says he believes it's important that Afghan parents support and encourage their children to follow their dreams, instead of limiting them. This will make children happier and more successful and, he believes, it will make their parents happier too.

Sitara Attaie is an actor and also a dancer, choreographer, model and linguist. In an interview with Edward Zellem (writer of Zarbul Masalha) she describes being part of the Afghan diaspora as a three-part process. The first stage is leaving everything behind, which is extremely difficult in itself. The second stage is the journey, which costs some Afghans their lives, and leaves others with lifelong trauma. But the third, toughest and longest stage is the process of integration in a new society, culture and language. Sitara suggests that while difficult, this part of the process offers opportunities and exciting challenges too.

Identity and Integration

For this piece, I interviewed three Afghan women: Elaha Walizadeh, a young woman born and raised outside Afghanistan who is now a university student, Sodaba Haidara, a journalism student in London, and Vida Afshar who lives in New Zealand having moved there from Afghanistan at the age of ten. How did they feel about their own personal journey of integration, what were the challenges and opportunities for them?

Themes emerged through the conversations. The first was the question of women's rights. For Elaha, having liberal parents, she says she has never experienced the cultural pressure of a conservative family: those Afghans who left Afghanistan years ago - around the time of Soviet occupation - have different values than those who left more recently. Elaha now defines herself as a feminist and activist, but she sometimes feels pulled in different ways. She would love to be more involved within the Afghan community where she lives – but also feels repelled by what strikes her as narrow-mindedness. "As a feminist activist I would disagree with so many things Afghans do and say and that's where the struggle lies. The struggle of being associated with your roots!"

Elaha also points out that there are misconceptions within Afghanistan about Afghan girls who have been living abroad. On her first and only trip to Afghanistan, Elaha felt she was perceived as a snob who didn't understand life struggles. She believes the Afghan media has played a role in creating these misconceptions. So, too, Elaha believes, are the bragging butchers and minicab drivers who have worked in London and return to Afghanistan to get married, claiming women in Europe are very bad. Perhaps their reaction is partly due to the unattainability of girls in the Afghan diaspora community. As Elaha's mother says: "No one who has lived all their life in Europe would get their educated daughters married to butchers, shopkeepers and cab drivers!"

Elaha believes education is the key solve this problem, which is not just about Afghans in Afghanistan compared to those elsewhere, but also within Afghan society. An educated person from Kabul, for example, does not have the same mindset as someone from a village.

Sodaba also feels pulled in different directions: she loves Afghan culture and traditions, but as an Afghan girl in the UK she also finds it hard to feel fully comfortable with them. She feels there is an expectation from people around her to 'behave like an Afghan girl'. As a student she joined the Afghan Student Society at her University, only to withdraw again when she noticed the mindset of most of the other members. For instance, when going for a meal together the girls sat separately from the guys, because they thought Afghan guys were very "shala", possessive and controlling. Sodaba disagrees with this judgmental attitude. She values her right to be different, to make her own choices, and wants neither to be dominated by Afghan culture nor to let other people's judgments affect her feelings about herself.

Sodaba has strong views about women's rights in society. When she visited Afghanistan last summer she says she felt people staring at her, as if they had never seen a woman before. Her jeans and blazers attracted too much attention. To lessen the attention she added a hijab and even stopped wearing her sunglasses. Sodaba describes Afghan society as a puzzle and limiting for women who are not supposed to laugh out loud, drive, run or raise their voices. Sodaba did drive anyway, but made peace with the other compromises she had to make during her stay in Afghanistan.

Feminism and women's rights is of great importance to Vida too. She experienced a hard transition between Afghan and Western culture when she moved to New Zealand. She was only ten years old and felt she had to stick to Sharia as a Muslim. In her teens her ideas began to change as she started studying women's rights in Islam, and soon discovered that men and women are given equal rights. She says that mullahs have misinterpreted the verses and this is the main reason why issues for women have arisen. Vida believes that mixing culture with religion means that neither gender is given equal rights. Our culture is very strict on women and in some ways it can be misinterpreted in teaching men to treat women as slaves, forcing men to believe it is stated in the Sharia.

Another important theme that emerged was that of belonging. Sodaba says she feels she does not fully blend in with British culture: She is literally in the middle of two cultures and to a certain extent has created a new identity of her own. When Sodaba and her family arrived in Britain her English was very weak, but her own curiosity and a good school made a big difference. British citizenship is mainly a piece of paper for her: "I remember going to my bank one time. I was inquiring about my statement so they asked a few security questions. They said, 'What's your nationality?' I said 'Afghan'. Their computer system obviously had me down as British so they declined to answer my questions because I had given the 'wrong' nationality."

Vida might be considered as being more into Afghan culture than that of New Zealand, the main reason being that she continues practicing and speaking her mother tongue, as she wants to be able to pass on her culture to future generations. Yet growing up in New Zealand has had a big impact on her feeling of identity. She has adapted to parts of the new culture, in sports, food and traditional dancing such as Kapa Haka. She finds that some aspects, like hospitality and kindness, are similar to Afghan culture. Vida describes Afghan culture as extremely hospitable which is something both fundamental and positive: "Peoples' kindness is absolutely admirable and something to be proud. Despite living in a state of war for decades, their hopes are still high, their hearts are still warm and welcoming."

When East meets West

The other theme that emerged in the conversations was that of mixed marriages, which is a hot topic

among the Afghan diaspora. Elaha's opinion on mixed
marriages, Afghans with non-Afghans in a British
society, is that they should be fine and not
condemned. Sodaba is in favour of mixed marriages
although she says she would prefer an Afghan
husband herself. Her friends who married non–
Afghans are happy, she says, as long as the person is
Muslim. Her only concern is that children might get
stuck between different cultures – whereas she feels
that one culture has to dominate. Vida's views on
marriage are complex. She thinks that arranged
marriages in Afghanistan are very upsetting when
they violate women's rights, but believes that
intercultural marriages between Afghans and non-
Afghans mostly end up in divorce, especially if the
couples date or have a physical relationship before
marriage. She believes that if cultural differences
cannot be bridged, the marriage will not succeed.

In my work and social life I regularly meet
Afghans in cross-cultural marriages. An Afghan
family is, 9.9 times out of 10, problematic about a
cross-cultural marriage, at least at the beginning.
Things might be easier if both people are of the same
faith. It seems more difficult for an Afghan woman to
marry a non-Afghan man than it is for an Afghan man
to marry a non-Afghan woman. Some of the concerns
parents in cross-cultural marriages have are that
their children will become confused when they reach
puberty, go off the rails, or reject their Afghan roots
and culture altogether. Yet, at the other end of the
spectrum, some parents are proud their children only
speak English. I have heard stories of arranged
marriages falling apart when the women becomes
more westernized after migrating to the West, and I

have heard other friends talk positively about their cross-cultural marriage and the benefits for their children of growing up with different influences and languages. There is no easy formula.

I am just Afghan, not a suicide bomber

What I experienced as an Afghan man in the UK is not just about our own struggles between two different cultures, or adjusting to a new society with questions about identity and belonging. I also believe that the host society has to overcome its fear of the new and the strange. I manage because I can deal with differences consciously. I knew what to expect in the West and have a decent package of world knowledge. Of course some of my expectations were wrong, but due to my ability to analyse and plan I am able to adjust and take on challenges, without damaging myself. This does not mean everything always goes smoothly for me - far from it - but I am able to deal with it, learn and grow.

When I was trying to set up a new life in the UK I was confronted with a lot of prejudice from institutions as well as individuals, and even grass roots organisations. I would like to make clear this is an institutionalized prejudice, rather than something within people. Basically British institutions have a lot of distrust towards migrants. A lot of what you say is questioned: your age, your migration reasons, and later your legal status, your education. You have to prove yourself continuously, whether it is for the migration process, for work, or for study. You get the impression that they regard Britain as the top of the world, the best of the best, and believe that every single person from outside the UK wants to live and profit from this paradise. For many migrants, nothing is further from the truth. I left my country because I had to, not because of greed. We love our 'watan', the extremely beautiful wilderness, the perfect seasons, strong traditions and rich cultural history, not to mention the delicious food. Replacing this with four wet seasons, individualistic London, pub and clubbing culture and bangers and mash is not always attractive.

When you tell British people you are an Afghan, a Pashtun, they seem to think of scary bearded men with AK47s and suicide vests, beating up their Burka-wearing, illiterate wives and breeding like crazy. The stereotype is far removed from the truth. Every Afghan man, for example, listens to his mother. You really don't want to patronize Afghan women: trust me, it won't end well for you. While we may have many children, that is because of the higher child mortality rate.

One of my experiences in my first days in Britain was that I was denied the chance to give an information evening about Afghanistan at a social centre. My posters were torn down and leaflets removed. The support I expected from a grass roots social organisation didn't materialise, which was not just disappointing, but also something I realised I simply had to accept without question. Not regarding myself as a helpless and dependent migrant, but rather a proud Afghan, didn't help.

The prejudice goes further, beyond my individual experience. As an Afghan organisation we have had difficulties finding funding, which we believe are due to stereotyping. Having the word 'Afghan' in your organisation seems to mean you go through more unnecessary paperwork than other organisations in the process of selection and beyond. I don't mind as long as I get the funding, because the bigger picture is to help develop our community in Britain towards positive social change and better integration with wider British society.

The overall effect, though, is that you feel that your identity as an Afghan is being stigmatized. It's as if you are not allowed to be who you are. I worry that these attitudes only increase confusion around the issue of identity and serve to enlarge the gap between communities instead of bridging them. However, I do not feel negative. On the contrary, I have learned a huge amount about a different part of the world on so many levels, have made new friends and met new people, for which I am very thankful. The British have a really good sense of humour and I am sure, with the passage of time, Britain will become my second home.

Conclusion

Lorna Stephenson

If, as Nina Yeo pointed out in her chapter on resilience, there is a danger of overshadowing the wealth of life experience of refugees by focusing only on asylum challenges, we hope this project has gone some way to counteract that tendency. Beneath the harsh realities of the asylum process, there are fascinating stories of lives spanning continents and cultures, such as those of Farah and Eleanor, and of the perseverance of those campaigning for the people they've left behind, such as Ivo and Robert. Other chapters sought to expose the system's bureaucracy, or demystify the trauma and mental health problems that can affect so many people. Throughout all the stories and articles featured is a thread of incredible human resilience. Perhaps most importantly for this project, we tried to create a forum where people of refugee and asylum seeker status can speak out within a context of society-imposed voicelessness.

The political background to refugee lives continues to get harder and more merciless. At the time of writing (April, 2014), the state of immigration politics is a telling snap-shot of the political climate. Along with the rise of the far-right UKIP, the Coalition government is silencing the publication of two reports - one on the impact of migrants on the labour market, and one on the indefinite detention of migrants - because their conclusions did not suit their agenda. The UK Border Force, which has been steadily increasing its ID controls on the streets and in workplaces, has recently been exposed as raiding workplaces without warrants.

The Immigration Bill is being debated in the House of Lords, on its alarmingly rapid route to royal assent. The bill will expand the already pervasive internal border system to include landlords, doctors and banks, who will face hefty fines should they serve undocumented people and make it their prerogative to vet customers and patients. It will, as the UN refugee agency has said, create a "climate of ethnic profiling" and the difficulties in establishing someone's status means "the provisions of the bill appear likely to result in asylum-seekers, refugees and beneficiaries of subsidiary protection being stigmatised in the public mind and in their being denied access to housing or bank accounts".

All in all, home secretary Theresa May continues full-throttle on her stated objective to make Britain a "hostile environment for illegal immigrants", a vague aim to please the right-wing press and satiate the xenophobic desires of anti-migrant groups. It ignores the fluidity of human experience beneath the state-imposed labels of legal status – 'refugee', 'asylum seeker', 'failed asylum seeker', 'illegal' – often arbitrary distinctions which serve only politicians and not those on which they are imposed. As Osman talking in Calais and Ivo and Robert writing from the UK demonstrated, status means nothing but its repercussions are severe. If this cruelty goes unchallenged, as Stephen posed in his essay, does this make us complicit? And when will we realise?

Thankfully, resistance is also growing. From the global level in international border zones to local initiatives in towns and cities across the UK, people are coming together to kick back against state-imposed racism and create new movements for solidarity regardless of origin, background or status.

In Calais, as in other EU border zones such as Lampedusa, Greece and Italy, a network of European citizens maintain a presence in support of the migrant communities. Activities span from providing humanitarian aid to standing with migrants to witness and document the police brutality doled out in the name of border security. But as immigration lawyer Francis Webber notes in her book Borderline Justice, "The legal, military, technological and diplomatic barriers to refugee movements are formidable. We need to up our game, finding creative ways to highlight and challenge the systematic closing off of routes to safety".

In the courts an active network of human rights and immigration lawyers are radically attentive to political developments and changes to immigration law, and challenge the injustice of legal developments through the courts and through lobbying. While a small number of MPs advocate for migrant rights in parliament, their influence is extremely limited in the face of the overwhelmingly negative and prejudicial attitude which informs the political status quo.

Perhaps most interesting and fertile are the community and grass roots efforts to welcome refugees and migrants, and campaign for a progressive, rights-based approach to migration policy. These efforts are diverse, from alternative media projects challenging stereotypes such as Refugee Radio, to open-to-all bike-fixing workshops and language classes.

Most detention centres in the UK have detention visiting groups working on the outside to arrange volunteer visitors to befriend individuals in detention. These groups are often also the first point of call for people in detention who need advice about the confusing, unknown situation they are thrust into when they are detained. One of the most established, Detention Action, which supports individuals in the Colnbrook and Harmondsworth Immigration Removal Centres, is also now an authoritative campaigning voice on detention matters.

Community centres, many run entirely by volunteers and self-funded through fund-raising and small grants, offer advice drop-ins in many cities in the UK. Such projects have become increasingly necessary since the cuts to legal aid for migrants and asylum seekers, and are often the only avenues available for people to seek independent advice on legal and welfare matters. Other more established projects have blossomed in recent years. The Unity Centre, located 100 metres from the reporting centre in Glasgow, is one example. As well as a drop-in service, the Centre offers reporting support. Their activities and premises have now expanded to include bike workshops, food distributions, film nights and much more. They run two charity shops to help support the projects.

The growth of these initiatives demonstrate what is perhaps the most important truth about the immigration debate. Despite the media vilification, and despite the political hostility, there is an undercurrent of friendship, empathy, hospitality and acceptance. Expanding this transformation from below is the best hope of halting the system's lurches into the darkness of racism and moral failure, and instead moving towards enlightened solidarity. To borrow Husnu's phrase, if we can fight for these rights, maybe we have a chance.

Biographical Information

Meriel Beattie studied French and German at Oxford. She started out as a journalist for Reuters in Eastern Europe just in time for the fall of the Soviet Union. She joined the BBC in 1993, working at the BBC World Service and as a reporter for Crossing Continents. Meriel has worked as a journalist around the world including several years in Turkey and Pakistan. She now lives in Brighton with her family.

Eleanor Clarke was born in Burma in 1933, the daughter of a Shan princess and a deputy commissioner in the Burma Frontier Service. She lived in Burma throughout the Second World War and the civil war which followed, before moving to Britain in 1958 to start a new life. Eleanor worked with blind veterans and then as a volunteer in mental health services. She has four children and ten grandchildren.

Gharghasht is an independent writer, blogger and a community broadcaster for the Afghan society in the United Kingdom. He founded Afghan Voice Radio and has developed it into a fully licensed independent community Internet radio station that also runs projects to help the community. He has worked as a specialist and consultant with national and international organizations in Afghanistan. He has been a Trustee of Refugee Radio since 2011.

Shawn Katz, Ph.D., is a Registered Counselling Psychologist with HCPC (Health and Care Professions Council), Chartered Counselling Psychologist and Associate Fellow with the BPS (British Psychological Society), Registered Psychotherapist with the UKCP (UK Council for Psychotherapists), and Accredited EMDR Consultant (EMDR UK& Ireland & EMDR Europe). Dr Katz held the post of specialist psychologist in an NHS Psychology Service in Brighton for nine years, and currently works as a Trauma Consultant and Supervisor for various NHS Trusts as well as in private practice in Brighton & Hove. He has specialized in the assessment and treatment of Post-Traumatic Stress Disorder and Complex Trauma including the Police, Fire Brigade, Military, refugees and victims of torture since 2000.

Ivo Kuka is a political activist from Cameroon who now lives in the UK with refugee status. In Cameroon and the UK, he has campaigned for human rights and

independence for Southern Cameroon. After fleeing
Cameroon due to persecution for his activities, Ivo
spent time in Harmondsworth Immigration Removal
Centre before being released to begin a new chapter
of his life. He now continues his political activities,
studies and volunteers, and is an outspoken critic of
immigration detention and the asylum process.

Husnu Koluman is a citizen of the world. He came
to the UK from Turkey and has lived in Germany. He
spent ten years waiting to learn if he could stay in the
UK before the Home Office granted him refugee
status. During that period the most important thing
that he learnt was to fight with difficulties. He is
interested in neurology, politics and economics and
hopes to find new ways to share his opinions with the
authorities and use scientific approaches to meet the
needs of humanity.

Farah Mohebati is a decorated volunteer and
community activist. She has recently received the
Special Impact Award in recognition of her work. She
is a founding Trustee of the Black and Minority
Ethnic Community Partnership and supports over 45
community groups including the Baha'i Community,
Sussex Interpreting Service, Refugee Radio, Mosaic,
the Migrant English Project and the International
Women's Committee. She left Iran for Brighton more
than 35 years ago and has never been back.

Derek Parkinson's interest in writing deepened with the arrival of the internet, and he has worked online as a journalist, copywriter and editor ever since. He is interested in how digital communications can change our lives, and has written about the impact of the Web on social inclusion, political engagement, and ways of improving public and private sector services. He has helped to set up fiction writing groups in Brighton and remains interested in supporting writers based in the city.

Stephen Silverwood is a charity worker and broadcaster. He studied at the University of Sussex and has an MA in Social Anthropology. He has worked with youth charities including the Children's Society and founded the children's literacy project, Upside Comics. He has worked with refugee communities in London and Brighton since 1999 and founded Refugee Radio in 2008.

Lorna Stephenson is a migrant rights campaigner and freelance journalist based in Brighton, who has spent time working with migrant projects in France and Morocco, along with solidarity projects in the UK. She is the editor of the Refugee Radio magazine and has previously written for Red Pepper, Corporate Watch and New Internationalist.

Robert Miki Tamanji is a lecturer from Cameroon. He is a life-long human rights activist and member of the Southern Cameroons National Council (SCNC).

After fleeing Cameroon due to persecution for his political activities, Robert experienced detention and impoverishment in the UK. He is still waiting for a decision on his asylum claim from the Home Office and lives in London with his family, where he continues to campaign for independence.

Nina Yeo has worked as a project manager and facilitator for peer-led, participatory projects with young people, refugees and those experiencing mental distress since 2006. She has been involved with the Resilience Panel since 2012. Nina is currently completing a PGDip in Mental Health Nursing, and writes poetry in her spare time